THE POETASTER
OR HIS ARRAIGNMENT

Ben Jonson

Contents

INTRODUCTION	7
ACT I	39
ACT II	56
ACT III	73
ACT IV	103
ACT V	137
GLOSSARY	189

THE POETASTER
OR HIS ARRAIGNMENT

BY
Ben Jonson

INTRODUCTION

THE greatest of English dramatists except Shakespeare, the first literary dictator and poet-laureate, a writer of verse, prose, satire, and criticism who most potently of all the men of his time affected the subsequent course of English letters: such was Ben Jonson, and as such his strong personality assumes an interest to us almost unparalleled, at least in his age.

Ben Jonson came of the stock that was centuries after to give to the world Thomas Carlyle; for Jonson's grandfather was of Annandale, over the Solway, whence he migrated to England. Jonson's father lost his estate under Queen Mary, "having been cast into prison and forfeited." He entered the church, but died a month before his illustrious son was born, leaving his widow and child in poverty. Jonson's birthplace was Westminster, and the time of his birth early in 1573. He was thus nearly ten years Shakespeare's junior, and less well off, if a trifle better born. But Jonson did not profit even by this slight advantage. His mother married beneath her, a wright or bricklayer, and Jonson was for a time apprenticed to the trade. As a youth he attracted the attention of the famous antiquary, William Camden, then usher at Westminster School, and there the poet laid the solid foundations of his classical learning. Jonson always held Camden in veneration, acknowledging that to him he owed,

"All that I am in arts, all that I know:"

and dedicating his first dramatic success, "Every Man in His Humour," to him. It is doubtful whether Jonson ever went to either university, though Fuller says that he was "statutably admitted into St. John's College, Cambridge." He tells us that he took no degree, but was later "Master of Arts in both the universities, by their favour, not his study." When a mere youth Jonson enlisted as a soldier trailing his pike in Flanders in the protracted wars of William the Silent against the Spanish. Jonson was a large and raw-boned lad; he became by his own account in time exceedingly bulky. In chat with his friend William Drummond of Hawthornden, Jonson told how "in his service in the Low Countries he had, in the face of both the camps, killed an enemy, and taken 'opima spolia' from him;" and how "since his coming to England, being appealed to the fields, he had killed his adversary which had hurt him in the arm and whose sword was ten inches longer than his." Jonson's reach may have made up for the lack of his sword; certainly his prowess lost nothing in the telling. Obviously Jonson was brave, combative, and not averse to talking of himself and his doings.

In 1592, Jonson returned from abroad penniless. Soon after he married, almost as early and quite as imprudently as Shakespeare. He told Drummond curtly that "his wife was a shrew, yet honest"; for some years he lived apart from her in the household of Lord Albany. Yet two touching epitaphs among Jonson's 'Epigrams', "On my first daughter," and "On my first son," attest the warmth of the poet's family affections. The daughter died in infancy, the son of the plague; another son grew up to manhood little credit to his father whom he survived. We know nothing beyond this of Jonson's domestic life.

How soon Jonson drifted into what we now call grandly "the theatrical profession" we do not know. In 1593 Marlowe made his tragic exit from life, and Greene, Shakespeare's other rival on the popular stage, had preceded Marlowe in an equally miserable death the year before. Shakespeare already had the running to himself. Jonson appears first in the employment of Philip Henslowe, the exploiter of several troupes of players, manager, and father-in-law of the famous actor, Edward Alleyn. From entries in 'Henslowe's Diary', a species of theatrical account book which has been handed down to us, we know that Jonson was connected with the Admiral's men; for he borrowed £4 of Henslowe, July 28, 1597, paying back 3s. 9d. on the same day on account of his "share" (in what is not altogether clear); while later, on December 3, of the same year, Henslowe advanced 20s. to him "upon a book which he showed the plot unto the company which he promised to deliver unto the company at Christmas next." In the next August Jonson was in collaboration with Chettle and Porter in a play called "Hot Anger Soon Cold." All this points to an association with Henslowe of some duration, as no mere tyro would be thus paid in advance upon mere promise. From allusions in Dekker's play, "Satiromastix," it appears that Jonson, like Shakespeare, began life as an actor, and that he "ambled in a leather pitch by a play-wagon" taking at one time the part of Hieronimo in Kyd's famous play, "The Spanish Tragedy." By the beginning of 1598, Jonson, though still in needy circumstances, had begun to receive recognition. Francis Meres--well known for his "Comparative Discourse of our English Poets with the Greek, Latin, and Italian Poets," printed in 1598, and for his mention therein of a dozen plays of Shakespeare by title --accords to Ben Jonson a place as one of "our best in tragedy," a matter of some surprise, as no known tragedy of Jonson from so early a date has come down to us. That Jonson was at work on tragedy, however, is proved by the entries in Henslowe of at least three tragedies, now lost, in which he had a hand. These are "Page of Plymouth," "King Robert II. of Scotland," and "Richard Crookback." But all of these came later, on his return to Henslowe, and range from August 1599 to June 1602.

Returning to the autumn of 1598, an event now happened to sever for a time Jonson's relations with Henslowe. In a letter to Alleyn, dated September 26 of that year, Henslowe writes: "I have lost one of my company that hurteth me greatly; that is Gabriel [Spencer], for he is slain in Hogsden fields by the hands of Benjamin Jonson, bricklayer." The last word is perhaps Henslowe's thrust at Jonson in his displeasure rather than a designation of his actual continuance at his trade up to this time. It is fair to Jonson to remark however, that his adversary appears to have been a notorious fire-eater who had shortly before killed one Feeke in a similar squabble. Duelling was a frequent occurrence of the time among gentlemen and the nobility; it was an imprudent breach of the peace on the part of a player. This duel is the one which Jonson described years after to Drummond, and for it Jonson was duly arraigned at Old Bailey, tried, and convicted. He was sent to prison and such goods and chattels as he had "were forfeited." It is a thought to give one pause that, but for the ancient law permitting convicted felons to plead, as it was called, the benefit of clergy, Jonson might have been hanged for this deed. The circumstance that the poet could read and write saved him; and he received only a brand of the letter "T," for Tyburn, on his left thumb. While in jail Jonson became a Roman Catholic; but he returned to the faith of the Church of England a dozen years later.

On his release, in disgrace with Henslowe and his former associates, Jonson offered his services as a playwright to Henslowe's rivals, the Lord Chamberlain's company, in which Shakespeare was a prominent shareholder. A tradition of long standing, though not susceptible of proof in a court of law, narrates that Jonson had submitted the manuscript of "Every Man in His Humour" to the Chamberlain's men and had received from the company a refusal; that Shakespeare called him back, read the play himself, and at once accepted it. Whether this story is true or not, certain it is that "Every Man in His Humour" was accepted by Shakespeare's company and acted for the first time in 1598, with Shakespeare taking a part. The evidence of this is contained in the list of actors prefixed to the comedy in the folio of Jonson's works, 1616. But it is a mistake to infer, because Shakespeare's name stands first in the list of actors and the elder Kno'well first in the 'dramatis personae', that Shakespeare took that particular part. The order of a list of Elizabethan players was generally that of their importance or priority as shareholders in the company and seldom if ever corresponded to the list of characters.

"Every Man in His Humour" was an immediate success, and with it Jonson's reputation as one of the leading dramatists of his time was established once and for all. This could have been by no means Jonson's earliest comedy, and we have just learned that he was already reputed one of "our best in tragedy." Indeed, one of Jonson's extant comedies, "The Case is Altered," but one never claimed by him or published as his, must certainly have preceded "Every Man in His Humour" on the stage. The former play may be described as a comedy modelled on the Latin plays of Plautus. (It combines, in fact, situations derived from the "Captivi" and the "Aulularia" of that dramatist). But the pretty story of the beggar-maiden, Rachel, and her suitors, Jonson found, not among the classics, but in the ideals of romantic love which Shakespeare had already popularised on the stage. Jonson never again produced so fresh and lovable a feminine personage as Rachel, although in other respects "The Case is Altered" is not a conspicuous play, and, save for the satirising of Antony Munday in the person of Antonio Balladino and Gabriel Harvey as well, is perhaps the least characteristic of the comedies of Jonson.

"Every Man in His Humour," probably first acted late in the summer of 1598 and at the Curtain, is commonly regarded as an epoch-making play; and this view is not unjustified. As to plot, it tells little more than how an intercepted letter enabled a father to follow his supposedly studious son to London, and there observe his life with the gallants of the time. The real quality of this comedy is in its personages and in the theory upon which they are conceived. Ben Jonson had theories about poetry and the drama, and he was neither chary in talking of them nor in experimenting with them in his plays. This makes Jonson, like Dryden in his time, and Wordsworth much later, an author to reckon with; particularly when we remember that many of Jonson's notions came for a time definitely to prevail and to modify the whole trend of English poetry. First of all Jonson was a classicist, that is, he believed in restraint and precedent in art in opposition to the prevalent ungoverned and irresponsible Renaissance spirit. Jonson believed that there was a professional way of doing things which might be reached by a study of the best examples, and he found these examples for the most part among the ancients. To confine our attention to the drama, Jonson objected to the amateurishness and haphazard nature of many contemporary plays, and set himself to do something different; and the first and most striking thing that he evolved was his conception and practice of the comedy of humours.

As Jonson has been much misrepresented in this matter, let us quote his own words as to "humour." A humour, according to Jonson, was a bias of disposition, a warp, so to speak, in character by which

> "Some one peculiar quality
> Doth so possess a man, that it doth draw
> All his affects, his spirits, and his powers,
> In their conflucions, all to run one way."

But continuing, Jonson is careful to add:

> "But that a rook by wearing a pied feather,
> The cable hat-band, or the three-piled ruff,
> A yard of shoe-tie, or the Switzers knot
> On his French garters, should affect a humour!
> O, it is more than most ridiculous."

Jonson's comedy of humours, in a word, conceived of stage personages on the basis of a ruling trait or passion (a notable simplification of actual life be it observed in passing); and, placing these typified traits in juxtaposition in their conflict and contrast, struck the spark of comedy. Downright, as his name indicates, is "a plain squire"; Bobadill's humour is that of the braggart who is incidentally, and with delightfully comic effect, a coward; Brainworm's humour is the finding out of things to the end of fooling everybody: of course he is fooled in the end himself. But it was not Jonson's theories alone that made the success of "Every Man in His Humour." The play is admirably written and each character is vividly conceived, and with a firm touch based on observation of the men of the London of the day. Jonson was neither in this, his first great comedy (nor in any other play that he wrote), a supine classicist, urging that English drama return to a slavish adherence to classical conditions. He says as to the laws of the old comedy (meaning by "laws," such matters as the unities of time and place and the use of chorus): "I see not then, but we should enjoy the same licence, or free power to illustrate and heighten our invention as they [the ancients] did; and not be tied to those strict and regular forms which the niceness of a few, who are nothing but form, would thrust upon us." "Every Man in His Humour" is written in prose, a novel practice which Jonson had of his predecessor in comedy, John Lyly. Even the word "humour" seems to have been employed in the Jonsonian sense by Chapman before Jonson's use of it. Indeed, the comedy of humours itself is only a heightened variety of the comedy of manners which represents life, viewed at a satirical angle, and is the oldest and most persistent species of comedy in the language. None the less, Jonson's comedy merited its immediate success and marked out a definite course in which comedy long continued to run. To mention only Shakespeare's Falstaff and his rout, Bardolph, Pistol, Dame Quickly, and the rest, whether in "Henry IV." or in "The Merry Wives of Windsor," all are conceived in the spirit of humours. So are the captains, Welsh, Scotch, and Irish of "Henry V.," and Malvolio especially later; though Shakespeare never employed the method of humours for an important personage. It was not Jonson's fault that many of his successors did precisely the thing that he had reprobated, that is, degrade "the humour: into an oddity of speech, an eccentricity of manner, of dress, or cut of beard. There was an anonymous play called "Every Woman in Her Humour." Chapman wrote "A Humourous Day's Mirth," Day, "Humour Out of Breath," Fletcher later, "The Humourous Lieutenant," and Jonson, besides "Every Man Out of His Humour," returned to the title in closing the cycle of his comedies in "The Magnetic Lady or Humours Reconciled."

With the performance of "Every Man Out of His Humour" in 1599, by Shakespeare's company once more at the Globe, we turn a new page in Jonson's career. Despite his many real virtues, if there is one feature more than any other that distinguishes Jonson, it is his arrogance; and to this may be added his self-righteousness, especially under criticism or satire. "Every Man Out of His Humour" is the first of three "comical satires" which Jonson contributed to what Dekker called the 'poetomachia' or war of the theatres as recent critics have named it. This play as a fabric of plot is a very slight affair; but as a satirical picture of the manners of the time, proceeding by means of vivid caricature, couched in witty and brilliant dialogue and sustained by that righteous indignation which must lie at the heart of all true satire--as a realisation, in short, of the classical ideal of comedy--there had been nothing like Jonson's comedy since the days of Aristophanes. "Every Man in His Humour," like the two plays that follow it, contains two kinds of attack, the critical or generally satiric, levelled at abuses and corruptions in the abstract; and the personal, in which specific application is made of all this in the lampooning of poets and others, Jonson's contemporaries. The method of personal attack by actual caricature of a person on the stage is almost as old as the drama. Aristophanes so lampooned Euripides in "The Acharnians" and Socrates in "The Clouds," to mention no other examples; and in English drama this kind of thing is alluded to again and again. What Jonson really did, was to raise the dramatic lampoon to an art, and make out of a casual burlesque and bit of mimicry a dramatic satire of literary pretensions and permanency. With the arrogant attitude mentioned above and his uncommon eloquence in scorn, vituperation, and invective, it is no wonder that Jonson soon involved himself in literary and even personal quarrels with his fellow-authors. The circumstances of the origin of this 'poetomachia' are far from clear, and those who have written on the topic, except of late, have not helped to make them clearer. The origin of the "war" has been referred to satirical references, apparently to Jonson, contained in "The Scourge of Villainy," a satire in regular form after the manner of the ancients by John Marston, a fellow playwright, subsequent friend and collaborator of Jonson's. On the other hand, epigrams of Jonson have been discovered (49, 68, and 100) variously charging "playwright" (reasonably identified with Marston) with scurrility, cowardice, and plagiarism; though the dates of the epigrams cannot be ascertained with certainty. Jonson's own statement of the matter to Drummond runs: "He had many quarrels with Marston, beat him, and took his pistol from him, wrote his 'Poetaster' on him; the beginning[s] of them were that Marston represented him on the stage."*[1]

Here at least we are on certain ground; and the principals of the quarrel are known. "Histriomastix," a play revised by Marston in 1598, has been regarded as the one in which Jonson was thus "represented on the stage"; although the personage in question, Chrisogonus, a poet, satirist, and translator, poor but proud, and contemptuous of the common herd, seems rather a complimentary portrait of Jonson than a caricature. As to the personages actually ridiculed in "Every Man Out of His Humour," Carlo Buffone was formerly thought certainly to be Marston, as he was described as "a public scurrilous, and profane jester," and elsewhere as the grand scourge or second untruss [that is, satirist], of the time" (Joseph Hall being by his own boast the first, and Marston's work being entitled "The Scourge of Villainy"). Apparently we must now prefer for Carlo a notorious character named Charles Chester, of whom gossipy and inaccurate Aubrey relates that he was "a bold impertinent fellow. . .a perpetual talker and made a noise like a drum in a room. So one time at a tavern Sir Walter Raleigh beats him and seals up his mouth (that is his upper and nether beard) with hard wax. From him Ben Jonson takes his Carlo Buffone ['i.e.', jester] in 'Every Man in His Humour' ['sic']." Is it conceivable that after all Jonson was ridiculing Marston, and that the point of the satire consisted in an intentional confusion of "the grand scourge or second untruss" with "the scurrilous and profane" Chester?

---

1 *The best account of this whole subject is to be found in the edition of 'Poetaster' and 'Satiromastix' by J. H. Penniman in 'Belles Lettres Series' shortly to appear. See also his earlier work, 'The War of the Theatres', 1892, and the excellent contributions to the subject by H. C. Hart in 'Notes and Queries', and in his edition of Jonson, 1906.

We have digressed into detail in this particular case to exemplify the difficulties of criticism in its attempts to identify the allusions in these forgotten quarrels. We are on sounder ground of fact in recording other manifestations of Jonson's enmity. In "The Case is Altered" there is clear ridicule in the character Antonio Balladino of Anthony Munday, pageant-poet of the city, translator of romances and playwright as well. In "Every Man in His Humour" there is certainly a caricature of Samuel Daniel, accepted poet of the court, sonneteer, and companion of men of fashion. These men held recognised positions to which Jonson felt his talents better entitled him; they were hence to him his natural enemies. It seems almost certain that he pursued both in the personages of his satire through "Every Man Out of His Humour," and "Cynthia's Revels," Daniel under the characters Fastidious Brisk and Hedon, Munday as Puntarvolo and Amorphus; but in these last we venture on quagmire once more. Jonson's literary rivalry of Daniel is traceable again and again, in the entertainments that welcomed King James on his way to London, in the masques at court, and in the pastoral drama. As to Jonson's personal ambitions with respect to these two men, it is notable that he became, not pageant-poet, but chronologer to the City of London; and that, on the accession of the new king, he came soon to triumph over Daniel as the accepted entertainer of royalty.

"Cynthia's Revels," the second "comical satire," was acted in 1600, and, as a play, is even more lengthy, elaborate, and impossible than "Every Man Out of His Humour." Here personal satire seems to have absorbed everything, and while much of the caricature is admirable, especially in the detail of witty and trenchantly satirical dialogue, the central idea of a fountain of self-love is not very well carried out, and the persons revert at times to abstractions, the action to allegory. It adds to our wonder that this difficult drama should have been acted by the Children of Queen Elizabeth's Chapel, among them Nathaniel Field with whom

Jonson read Horace and Martial, and whom he taught later how to make plays. Another of these precocious little actors was Salathiel Pavy, who died before he was thirteen, already famed for taking the parts of old men. Him Jonson immortalised in one of the sweetest of his epitaphs. An interesting sidelight is this on the character of this redoubtable and rugged satirist, that he should thus have befriended and tenderly remembered these little theatrical waifs, some of whom (as we know) had been literally kidnapped to be pressed into the service of the theatre and whipped to the conning of their difficult parts. To the caricature of Daniel and Munday in "Cynthia's Revels" must be added Anaides (impudence), here assuredly Marston, and Asotus (the prodigal), interpreted as Lodge or, more perilously, Raleigh. Crites, like Asper-Macilente in "Every Man Out of His Humour," is Jonson's self-complaisant portrait of himself, the just, wholly admirable, and judicious scholar, holding his head high above the pack of the yelping curs of envy and detraction, but careless of their puny attacks on his perfections with only too mindful a neglect.

The third and last of the "comical satires" is "Poetaster," acted, once more, by the Children of the Chapel in 1601, and Jonson's only avowed contribution to the fray. According to the author's own account, this play was written in fifteen weeks on a report that his enemies had entrusted to Dekker the preparation of "Satiromastix, the Untrussing of the Humorous Poet," a dramatic attack upon himself. In this attempt to forestall his enemies Jonson succeeded, and "Poetaster" was an immediate and deserved success. While hardly more closely knit in structure than its earlier companion pieces, "Poetaster" is planned to lead up to the ludicrous final scene in which, after a device borrowed from the "Lexiphanes" of Lucian, the offending poetaster, Marston-Crispinus, is made to throw up the difficult words with which he had overburdened his stomach as well as overlarded his vocabulary. In the end Crispinus with his fellow, Dekker-Demetrius, is bound over to keep the peace and never thenceforward "malign, traduce, or detract the person or writings of Quintus Horatius Flaccus [Jonson] or any other eminent man transcending you in merit." One of the most diverting personages in Jonson's comedy is Captain Tucca. "His peculiarity" has been well described by Ward as "a buoyant blackguardism which recovers itself instantaneously from the most complete exposure, and a picturesqueness of speech like that of a walking dictionary of slang."

It was this character, Captain Tucca, that Dekker hit upon in his reply, "Satiromastix," and he amplified him, turning his abusive vocabulary back upon Jonson and adding "An immodesty to his dialogue that did not enter into Jonson's conception." It has been held, altogether plausibly, that when Dekker was engaged professionally, so to speak, to write a dramatic reply to Jonson, he was at work on a species of chronicle history, dealing with the story of Walter Terill in the reign of William Rufus. This he hurriedly adapted to include the satirical characters suggested by "Poetaster," and fashioned to convey the satire of his reply. The absurdity of placing Horace in the court of a Norman king is the result. But Dekker's play is not without its palpable hits at the arrogance, the literary pride, and self-righteousness of Jonson-Horace, whose "ningle" or pal, the absurd Asinius Bubo, has recently been shown to figure forth, in all likelihood, Jonson's friend, the poet Drayton. Slight and hastily adapted as is "Satiromastix," especially in a comparison with the better wrought and more significant satire of "Poetaster," the town awarded the palm to Dekker, not to Jonson; and Jonson gave over in consequence his practice of "comical satire." Though Jonson was cited to appear before the Lord Chief Justice to answer certain charges to the effect that he had attacked lawyers and soldiers in "Poetaster," nothing came of this complaint. It may be suspected that much of this furious clatter and give-and-take was pure playing to the gallery. The town was agog with the strife, and on no less an authority than Shakespeare ("Hamlet," ii. 2), we learn that the children's company (acting the plays of Jonson) did "so berattle the common stages. . .that many, wearing rapiers, are afraid of goose-quills, and dare scarce come thither."

Several other plays have been thought to bear a greater or less part in the war of the theatres. Among them the most important is a college play, entitled "The Return from Parnassus," dating 1601-02. In it a much-quoted passage makes Burbage, as a character, declare: "Why here's our fellow Shakespeare puts them all down; aye and Ben Jonson, too. O that Ben Jonson is a pestilent fellow; he brought up Horace, giving the poets a pill, but our fellow Shakespeare hath given him a purge that made him bewray his credit." Was Shakespeare then concerned in this war of the stages? And what could have been the nature of this "purge"? Among several suggestions, "Troilus and Cressida" has been thought by some to be the play in which Shakespeare thus "put down" his friend, Jonson. A wiser interpretation finds the "purge" in "Satiromastix," which, though not written by Shakespeare, was staged by his company, and therefore with his approval and under his direction as one of the leaders of that company.

The last years of the reign of Elizabeth thus saw Jonson recognised as a dramatist second only to Shakespeare, and not second even to him as a dramatic satirist. But Jonson now turned his talents to new fields. Plays on subjects derived from classical story and myth had held the stage from the beginning of the drama, so that Shakespeare was making no new departure when he wrote his "Julius Caesar" about 1600. Therefore when Jonson staged "Sejanus," three years later and with Shakespeare's company once more, he was only following in the elder dramatist's footsteps. But Jonson's idea of a play on classical history, on the one hand, and Shakespeare's and the elder popular dramatists, on the other, were very different. Heywood some years before had put five straggling plays on the stage in quick succession, all derived from stories in Ovid and dramatised with little taste or discrimination. Shakespeare had a finer conception of form, but even he was contented to take all his ancient history from North's translation of Plutarch and dramatise his subject without further inquiry. Jonson was a scholar and a classical antiquarian. He reprobated this slipshod amateurishness, and wrote his "Sejanus" like a scholar, reading Tacitus, Suetonius, and other authorities, to be certain of his facts, his setting, and his atmosphere, and somewhat pedantically noting his authorities in the margin when he came to print. "Sejanus" is a tragedy of genuine dramatic power in which is told with discriminating taste the story of the haughty favourite of Tiberius with his tragical overthrow. Our drama presents no truer nor more painstaking representation of ancient Roman life than may be found in Jonson's "Sejanus" and "Catiline his Conspiracy," which followed in 1611. A passage in the address of the former play to the reader, in which Jonson refers to a collaboration in an earlier version, has led to the surmise that Shakespeare may have been that "worthier pen." There is no evidence to determine the matter.

In 1605, we find Jonson in active collaboration with Chapman and Marston in the admirable comedy of London life entitled "Eastward Hoe." In the previous year, Marston had dedicated his "Malcontent," in terms of fervid admiration, to Jonson; so that the wounds of the war of the theatres must have been long since healed. Between Jonson and Chapman there was the kinship of similar scholarly ideals. The two continued friends throughout life. "Eastward Hoe" achieved the extraordinary popularity represented in a demand for three issues in one year. But this was not due entirely to the merits of the play. In its earliest version a passage which an irritable courtier conceived to be derogatory to his nation, the Scots, sent both Chapman and Jonson to jail; but the matter was soon patched up, for by this time Jonson had influence at court.

With the accession of King James, Jonson began his long and successful career as a writer of masques. He wrote more masques than all his competitors together, and they are of an extraordinary variety and poetic excellence. Jonson did not invent the masque; for such premeditated devices to set and frame, so to speak, a court ball had been known and practised in varying degrees of elaboration long before his time. But Jonson gave dramatic value to the masque, especially in his invention of the antimasque, a comedy or farcical element of relief, entrusted to professional players or dancers. He enhanced, as well, the beauty and dignity of those portions of the masque in which noble lords and ladies took their parts to create, by their gorgeous costumes and artistic grouping and evolutions, a sumptuous show. On the mechanical and scenic side Jonson had an inventive and ingenious partner in Inigo Jones, the royal architect, who more than any one man raised the standard of stage representation in the England of his day. Jonson continued active in the service of the court in the writing of masques and other entertainments far into the reign of King Charles; but, towards the end, a quarrel with Jones embittered his life, and the two testy old men appear to have become not only a constant irritation to each other, but intolerable bores at court.
In "Hymenaei," "The Masque of Queens," "Love Freed from Ignorance," "Lovers made Men," "Pleasure Reconciled to Virtue," and many more will be found Jonson's aptitude, his taste, his poetry and inventiveness in these by-forms of the drama; while in "The Masque of Christmas," and "The Gipsies Metamorphosed" especially, is discoverable that power of broad comedy which, at court as well as in the city, was not the least element of Jonson's contemporary

popularity.

But Jonson had by no means given up the popular stage when he turned to the amusement of King James. In 1605 "Volpone" was produced, "The Silent Woman" in 1609, "The Alchemist" in the following year. These comedies, with "Bartholomew Fair," 1614, represent Jonson at his height, and for constructive cleverness, character successfully conceived in the manner of caricature, wit and brilliancy of dialogue, they stand alone in English drama. "Volpone, or the Fox," is, in a sense, a transition play from the dramatic satires of the war of the theatres to the purer comedy represented in the plays named above. Its subject is a struggle of wit applied to chicanery; for among its 'dramatis personae', from the villainous Fox himself, his rascally servant Mosca, Voltore (the vulture), Corbaccio and Corvino (the big and the little raven), to Sir Politic Would-be and the rest, there is scarcely a virtuous character in the play. Question has been raised as to whether a story so forbidding can be considered a comedy, for, although the plot ends in the discomfiture and imprisonment of the most vicious, it involves no moral catastrophe. But Jonson was on sound historical ground, for "Volpone" is conceived far more logically on the lines of the ancients' theory of comedy than was ever the romantic drama of Shakespeare, however repulsive we may find a philosophy of life that facilely divides the world into the rogues and their dupes, and, identifying brains with roguery and innocence with folly, admires the former while inconsistently punishing them.

"The Silent Woman" is a gigantic farce of the most ingenious construction. The whole comedy hinges on a huge joke, played by a heartless nephew on his misanthropic uncle, who is induced to take to himself a wife, young, fair, and warranted silent, but who, in the end, turns out neither silent nor a woman at all. In "The

Alchemist," again, we have the utmost cleverness in construction, the whole fabric building climax on climax, witty, ingenious, and so plausibly presented that we forget its departures from the possibilities of life. In "The Alchemist" Jonson represented, none the less to the life, certain sharpers of the metropolis, revelling in their shrewdness and rascality and in the variety of the stupidity and wickedness of their victims. We may object to the fact that the only person in the play possessed of a scruple of honesty is discomfited, and that the greatest scoundrel of all is approved in the end and rewarded. The comedy is so admirably written and contrived, the personages stand out with such lifelike distinctness in their several kinds, and the whole is animated with such verve and resourcefulness that "The Alchemist" is a new marvel every time it is read. Lastly of this group comes the tremendous comedy, "Bartholomew Fair," less clear cut, less definite, and less structurally worthy of praise than its three predecessors, but full of the keenest and cleverest of satire and inventive to a degree beyond any English comedy save some other of Jonson's own. It is in "Bartholomew Fair" that we are presented to the immortal caricature of the Puritan, Zeal-in-the-Land Busy, and the Littlewits that group about him, and it is in this extraordinary comedy that the humour of Jonson, always open to this danger, loosens into the Rabelaisian mode that so delighted King James in "The Gipsies Metamorphosed." Another comedy of less merit is "The Devil is an Ass," acted in 1616. It was the failure of this play that caused Jonson to give over writing for the public stage for a period of nearly ten years.

"Volpone" was laid as to scene in Venice. Whether because of the success of "Eastward Hoe" or for other reasons, the other three comedies declare in the words of the prologue to "The Alchemist":

"Our scene is London, 'cause we would make known

No country's mirth is better than our own."

Indeed Jonson went further when he came to revise his plays for collected publication in his folio of 1616, he transferred the scene of "Every Man in His Humour" from Florence to London also, converting Signior Lorenzo di Pazzi to Old Kno'well, Prospero to Master Welborn, and Hesperida to Dame Kitely "dwelling i' the Old Jewry."

In his comedies of London life, despite his trend towards caricature, Jonson has shown himself a genuine realist, drawing from the life about him with an experience and insight rare in any generation. A happy comparison has been suggested between Ben Jonson and Charles Dickens. Both were men of the people, lowly born and hardly bred. Each knew the London of his time as few men knew it; and each represented it intimately and in elaborate detail. Both men were at heart moralists, seeking the truth by the exaggerated methods of humour and caricature; perverse, even wrong-headed at times, but possessed of a true pathos and largeness of heart, and when all has been said--though the Elizabethan ran to satire, the Victorian to sentimentality--leaving the world better for the art that they practised in it.

In 1616, the year of the death of Shakespeare, Jonson collected his plays, his poetry, and his masques for publication in a collective edition. This was an unusual thing at the time and had been attempted by no dramatist before Jonson. This volume published, in a carefully revised text, all the plays thus far mentioned, excepting "The Case is Altered," which Jonson did not acknowledge, "Bartholomew Fair," and "The Devil is an Ass," which was written too late. It included likewise a book of some hundred and thirty odd 'Epigrams', in which form of brief and pungent writing Jonson was an acknowledged master; "The Forest," a smaller collection of lyric and occasional verse and some ten 'Masques' and 'Entertainments'. In this same year Jonson was made poet laureate with a pension of one hundred marks a year. This, with his fees and returns from several noblemen, and the small earnings of his plays must have formed the bulk of his income. The poet appears to have done certain literary hack-work for others, as, for example, parts of the Punic Wars contributed to Raleigh's 'History of the World'. We know from a story, little to the credit of either, that Jonson accompanied Raleigh's son abroad in the capacity of a tutor. In 1618 Jonson was granted the reversion of the office of Master of the Revels, a post for which he was peculiarly fitted; but he did not live to enjoy its perquisites. Jonson was honoured with degrees by both universities, though when and under what circumstances is not known. It has been said that he narrowly escaped the honour of knighthood, which the satirists of the day averred King James was wont to lavish with an indiscriminate hand. Worse men were made knights in his day than worthy Ben Jonson.

From 1616 to the close of the reign of King James, Jonson produced nothing for the stage. But he "prosecuted" what he calls "his wonted studies" with such assiduity that he became in reality, as by report, one of the most learned men of his time. Jonson's theory of authorship involved a wide acquaintance with books and "an ability," as he put it, "to convert the substance or riches of another poet to his own use." Accordingly Jonson read not only the Greek and Latin classics down to the lesser writers, but he acquainted himself especially with the Latin writings of his learned contemporaries, their prose as well as their poetry, their antiquities and curious lore as well as their more solid learning. Though a poor man, Jonson was an indefatigable collector of books. He told Drummond that "the Earl of Pembroke sent him £20 every first day of the new year to buy new books." Unhappily, in 1623, his library was destroyed by fire, an accident serio-comically described in his witty poem, "An Execration upon Vulcan." Yet even now a book turns up from time to time in which is inscribed, in fair large Italian lettering, the name, Ben Jonson. With respect to Jonson's use of his material, Dryden said memorably of him: "[He] was not only a professed imitator of Horace, but a learned plagiary of all the others; you track him everywhere in their snow. . . . But he has done his robberies so openly that one sees he fears not to be taxed by any law. He invades authors like a monarch, and what would be theft in other poets is only victory in him." And yet it is but fair to say that Jonson prided himself, and justly, on his originality. In "Catiline," he not only uses Sallust's account of the conspiracy, but he models some of the speeches of Cicero on the Roman orator's actual words. In "Poetaster," he lifts a whole satire out of Horace and dramatises it effectively for his purposes. The sophist Libanius suggests the situation of "The Silent Woman"; a Latin comedy of Giordano Bruno, "Il Candelaio," the relation of the dupes and the sharpers in "The Alchemist," the "Mostellaria" of Plautus, its admirable opening scene. But Jonson commonly bettered his sources, and putting the stamp of his sovereignty on whatever bullion he borrowed made it thenceforward to all time current and his own.

The lyric and especially the occasional poetry of Jonson has a peculiar merit. His theory demanded design and the perfection of literary finish. He was furthest from the rhapsodist and the careless singer of an idle day; and he believed that Apollo could only be worthily served in singing robes and laurel crowned. And yet many of Jonson's lyrics will live as long as the language. Who does not know "Queen and huntress, chaste and fair." "Drink to me only with thine eyes," or "Still to be neat, still to be dressed"? Beautiful in form, deft and graceful in expression, with not a word too much or one that bears not its part in the total effect, there is yet about the lyrics of Jonson a certain stiffness and formality, a suspicion that they were not quite spontaneous and unbidden, but that they were carved, so to speak, with disproportionate labour by a potent man of letters whose habitual thought is on greater things. It is for these reasons that Jonson is even better in the epigram and in occasional verse where rhetorical finish and pointed wit less interfere with the spontaneity and emotion which we usually associate with lyrical poetry. There are no such epitaphs as Ben Jonson's, witness the charming ones on his own children, on Salathiel Pavy, the child-actor, and many more; and this even though the rigid law of mine and thine must now restore to William Browne of Tavistock the famous lines beginning: "Underneath this sable hearse." Jonson is unsurpassed, too, in the difficult poetry of compliment, seldom falling into fulsome praise and disproportionate similtude, yet showing again and again a generous appreciation of worth in others, a discriminating taste and a generous personal regard. There was no man in England of his rank so well known and universally beloved as Ben Jonson. The list of his friends, of those to whom he had written verses, and those who had written verses to him, includes the name of every man of prominence in the England of King James. And the tone of many of these productions discloses an affectionate familiarity that speaks for the amiable personality and sound worth of the laureate. In 1619, growing unwieldy through inactivity, Jonson hit upon the heroic remedy of a journey afoot to Scotland. On his way thither and back he was hospitably received at the houses of many friends and by those to whom his friends had recommended him. When he arrived in Edinburgh, the burgesses met to grant him the freedom of the city, and Drummond, foremost of Scottish poets, was proud to entertain him for weeks as his guest at Hawthornden. Some of the noblest of Jonson's poems were inspired by friendship. Such is the fine "Ode to the memory of Sir Lucius Cary and Sir Henry Moryson," and that admirable piece of critical insight and filial affection, prefixed to the first

Shakespeare folio, "To the memory of my beloved master, William Shakespeare, and what he hath left us." to mention only these. Nor can the earlier "Epode," beginning "Not to know vice at all," be matched in stately gravity and gnomic wisdom in its own wise and stately age.

But if Jonson had deserted the stage after the publication of his folio and up to the end of the reign of King James, he was far from inactive; for year after year his inexhaustible inventiveness continued to contribute to the masquing and entertainment at court. In "The Golden Age Restored," Pallas turns from the Iron Age with its attendant evils into statues which sink out of sight; in "Pleasure Reconciled to Virtue," Atlas figures represented as an old man, his shoulders covered with snow, and Comus, "the god of cheer or the belly," is one of the characters, a circumstance which an imaginative boy of ten, named John Milton, was not to forget. "Pan's Anniversary," late in the reign of James, proclaimed that Jonson had not yet forgotten how to write exquisite lyrics, and "The Gipsies Metamorphosed" displayed the old drollery and broad humorous stroke still unimpaired and unmatchable. These, too, and the earlier years of Charles were the days of the Apollo Room of the Devil Tavern where Jonson presided, the absolute monarch of English literary Bohemia. We hear of a room blazoned about with Jonson's own judicious 'Leges Convivales' in letters of gold, of a company made up of the choicest spirits of the time, devotedly attached to their veteran dictator, his reminiscences, opinions, affections, and enmities. And we hear, too, of valorous potations; but in the words of Herrick addressed to his master, Jonson, at the Devil Tavern, as at the Dog, the Triple Tun, and at the Mermaid,

> "We such clusters had
> As made us nobly wild, not mad,
> And yet each verse of thine

Outdid the meat, outdid the frolic wine."

But the patronage of the court failed in the days of King Charles, though Jonson was not without royal favours; and the old poet returned to the stage, producing, between 1625 and 1633, "The Staple of News," "The New Inn," "The Magnetic Lady," and "The Tale of a Tub," the last doubtless revised from a much earlier comedy. None of these plays met with any marked success, although the scathing generalisation of Dryden that designated them "Jonson's dotages" is unfair to their genuine merits. Thus the idea of an office for the gathering, proper dressing, and promulgation of news (wild flight of the fancy in its time) was an excellent subject for satire on the existing absurdities among the newsmongers; although as much can hardly be said for "The Magnetic Lady," who, in her bounty, draws to her personages of differing humours to reconcile them in the end according to the alternative title, or "Humours Reconciled." These last plays of the old dramatist revert to caricature and the hard lines of allegory; the moralist is more than ever present, the satire degenerates into personal lampoon, especially of his sometime friend, Inigo Jones, who appears unworthily to have used his influence at court against the broken-down old poet. And now disease claimed Jonson, and he was bedridden for months. He had succeeded Middleton in 1628 as Chronologer to the City of London, but lost the post for not fulfilling its duties. King Charles befriended him, and even commissioned him to write still for the entertainment of the court; and he was not without the sustaining hand of noble patrons and devoted friends among the younger poets who were proud to be "sealed of the tribe of Ben."

Jonson died, August 6, 1637, and a second folio of his works, which he had been some time gathering, was printed in 1640, bearing in its various parts dates ranging from 1630 to 1642. It included all the plays mentioned in the foregoing paragraphs, excepting "The Case is Altered;" the masques, some fifteen, that date between 1617 and 1630; another collection of lyrics and occasional poetry called "Underwoods, including some further entertainments; a translation of "Horace's Art of Poetry" (also published in a vicesimo quarto in 1640), and certain fragments and ingatherings which the poet would hardly have included himself. These last comprise the fragment (less than seventy lines) of a tragedy called "Mortimer his Fall," and three acts of a pastoral drama of much beauty and poetic spirit, "The Sad Shepherd." There is also the exceedingly interesting 'English Grammar' "made by Ben Jonson for the benefit of all strangers out of his observation of the English language now spoken and in use," in Latin and English; and 'Timber, or discoveries' "made upon men and matter as they have flowed out of his daily reading, or had their reflux to his peculiar notion of the times." The 'Discoveries', as it is usually called, is a commonplace book such as many literary men have kept, in which their reading was chronicled, passages that took their fancy translated or transcribed, and their passing opinions noted. Many passage of Jonson's 'Discoveries' are literal translations from the authors he chanced to be reading, with the reference, noted or not, as the accident of the moment prescribed. At times he follows the line of Macchiavelli's argument as to the nature and conduct of princes; at others he clarifies his own conception of poetry and poets by recourse to Aristotle. He finds a choice paragraph on eloquence in Seneca the elder and applies it to his own recollection of Bacon's power as an orator; and another on facile and ready genius, and translates it, adapting it to his recollection of his fellow-playwright, Shakespeare. To call such passages--which Jonson never intended for publication--plagiarism, is to obscure the significance of words. To disparage his memory by citing them is a preposterous use of scholarship. Jonson's prose, both in his dramas, in the descriptive comments of his masques, and in the 'Discoveries', is characterised by clarity and vigorous directness, nor is it wanting in a fine sense of form or in the subtler graces of diction.

When Jonson died there was a project for a handsome monument to his memory. But the Civil War was at hand, and the project failed. A memorial, not insufficient, was carved on the stone covering his grave in one of the aisles of Westminster Abbey:

"O rare Ben Jonson."

FELIX E. SCHELLING.

THE COLLEGE, PHILADELPHIA, U.S.A.

TO THE VIRTUOUS, AND MY WORTHY FRIEND
       MR. RICHARD MARTIN

SIR,--A thankful man owes a courtesy ever; the unthankful but when he needs it. To make mine own mark appear, and shew by which of these seals I am known, I send you this piece of what may live of mine; for whose innocence, as for the author's, you were once a noble and timely undertaker, to the greatest justice of this kingdom. Enjoy now the delight of your goodness, which is, to see that prosper you preserved, and posterity to owe the reading of that, without offence, to your name, which so much ignorance and malice of the times then conspired to have supprest.
       Your true lover,   BEN JONSON.

DRAMATIS PERSONAE

AUGUSTUS CAESAR.	HERMOGENES TIGELLIUS.
MACAENUES.	DEMETRIUS FANNIUS.
MARC. OVID.	ALBIUS.
COR. GALLUS.	MINOS.
SEX. PROPERTIUS.	HISTRIO.
FUS. ARISTIUS.	AESOP.
PUB. OVID.	PYRGI.
VIRGIL.	Lictors, Equitis, etc. Horace.
TREBATIUS.	JULIA.
ASINIUS LUPUS.	CYTHERIS.
PANTILIUS TUCCA.	PLAUTIA.
LUSCUS.	CHLOE.
RUF. LAB. CRISPINUS.	Maids.

SCENE,-Rome

After the second sounding.
ENVY arises in the midst of the stage.

Light, I salute thee, but with wounded nerves,
Wishing the golden splendor pitchy darkness.
What's here? THE ARRAIGNMENT! ay; this, this is it,
That our sunk eyes have waked for all this while:
Here will be subject for my snakes and me.
Cling to my neck and wrists, my loving worms,
And cast you round in soft and amorous folds,
Till I do bid uncurl; then, break your knots,
Shoot out yourselves at length, as your forced stings
Would hide themselves within his maliced sides,
To whom I shall apply you. Stay! the shine
Of this assembly here offends my sight;
I'll darken that first, and outface their grace.
Wonder not, if I stare: these fifteen weeks,
So long as since the plot was but an embrion,
Have I, with burning lights mixt vigilant thoughts,
In expectation of this hated play,
To which at last I am arrived as Prologue.
Nor would I you should look for other looks,
Gesture, or compliment from me, than what
The infected bulk of Envy can afford:
For I am risse here with a covetous hope,

To blast your pleasures and destroy your sports,
With wrestings, comments, applications,
Spy-like suggestions, privy whisperings,
And thousand such promoting sleights as these.
Mark how I will begin: The scene is, ha!
Rome? Rome? and Rome? Crack, eye-strings, and your balls
Drop into earth; let me be ever blind.
I am prevented; all my hopes are crost,
Check'd, and abated; fie, a freezing sweat
Flows forth at all my pores, my entrails burn:
What should I do? Rome! Rome! O my vext soul,
How might I force this to the present state?
Are there no players here? no poet apes,
That come with basilisk's eyes, whose forked tongues
Are steeped in venom, as their hearts in gall?
Either of these would help me; they could wrest,
Pervert, and poison all they hear or see,
With senseless glosses, and allusions.
Now, if you be good devils, fly me not.
You know what dear and ample faculties
I have endowed you with: I'll lend you more.
Here, take my snakes among you, come and eat,
And while the squeez'd juice flows in your black jaws,
Help me to damn the author. Spit it forth
Upon his lines, and shew your rusty teeth
At every word, or accent: or else choose
Out of my longest vipers, to stick down
In your deep throats; and let the heads come forth
At your rank mouths; that he may see you arm'd
With triple malice, to hiss, sting, and tear.
His work and him; to forge, and then declaim,
Traduce, corrupt, apply, inform, suggest;
O, these are gifts wherein your souls are blest.

What? Do you hide yourselves? will none appear?
None answer? what, doth this calm troop affright you?
Nay, then I do despair; down, sink again:
This travail is all lost with my dead hopes.
If in such bosoms spite have left to dwell,
Envy is not on earth, nor scarce in hell.   [Descends slowly.

The third sounding.

[As she disappears, enter PROLOGUE hastily, in armour.

Stay, monster, ere thou sink-thus on thy head
Set we our bolder foot; with which we tread
Thy malice into earth: so Spite should die,
Despised and scorn'd by noble industry.
If any muse why I salute the stage,
An armed Prologue; know, 'tis a dangerous age:
Wherein who writes, had need present his scenes
Forty-fold proof against the conjuring means
Of base detractors, and illiterate apes,
That fill up rooms in fair and formal shapes.
'Gainst these, have we put on this forced defence:
Whereof the allegory and hid sense
Is, that a well erected confidence
Can fright their pride, and laugh their folly hence.
Here now, put case our author should, once more,
Swear that his play were good; he doth implore,
You would not argue him of arrogance:
Howe'er that common spawn of ignorance,
Our fry of writers, may beslime his fame,
And give his action that adulterate name.

Such full-blown vanity he more doth loth,
Than base dejection; there's a mean 'twixt both,
Which with a constant firmness he pursues,
As one that knows the strength of his own Muse.
And this he hopes all free souls will allow:
Others that take it with a rugged brow,
Their moods he rather pities than envies:
His mind it is above their injuries.

ACT I

SCENE 1--Scene draws, and discovers OVID in his study.

Ovid.
  Then, when this body falls in funeral fire,
  My name shall live, and my best part aspire.
  It shall go so.

        [Enter Luscus, with a gown and cap.

LUSC. Young master, master Ovid, do you hear? Gods a'me! away with your songs and sonnets and on with your gown and cap quickly: here, here, your father will be a man of this room presently. Come, nay, nay, nay, nay, be brief. These verses too, a poison on 'em! I cannot abide them, they make me ready to cast, by the banks of Helicon! Nay, look, what a rascally untoward thing this poetry is; I could tear them now.

Ovid. Give me; how near is my father?

Lusc. Heart a'man: get a law book in your hand, I will not answer you else. [Ovid puts on his cap and gown]. Why so! now there's some formality in you. By Jove, and three or four of the gods more,

I am right of mine old master's humour for that; this villainous poetry will undo you, by the welkin.

Ovid. What, hast thou buskins on, Luscus, that thou swearest so tragically and high?

Lusc. No, but I have boots on, sir, and so has your father too by this time; for he call'd for them ere I came from the lodging.

Ovid. Why, was he no readier?

Lusc. O no; and there was the mad skeldering captain, with the velvet arms, ready to lay hold on him as he comes down: he that presses every man he meets, with an oath to lend him money, and cries, Thou must do't, old boy, as thou art a man, a man of worship.

Ovid. Who, Pantilius Tucca?

Lus. Ay, he; and I met little master Lupus, the tribune, going thither too.

Ovid. Nay, an he be under their arrest, I may with safety enough read over my elegy before he come.

Lus. Gods a'me! what will you do? why, young master, you are not Castalian mad, lunatic, frantic, desperate, ha!

Ovid. What ailest thou, Luscus?

Lus. God be with you, sir; I'll leave you to your poetical fancies, and furies. I'll not be guilty, I.   [Exit.

Ovid.
> Be not, good ignorance. I'm glad th'art gone;
> For thus alone, our ear shall better judge
> The hasty errors of our morning muse.

> Envy, why twit'st thou me my time's spent ill,
> And call'st my verse, fruits of an idle quill?
> Or that, unlike the line from whence I sprung,
> War's dusty honours I pursue not young?
> Or that I study not the tedious laws,
> And prostitute my voice in every cause?
> Thy scope is mortal; mine eternal fame,
> Which through the world shall ever chaunt my name.
> Homer will live whilst Tenedos stands, and Ide,
> Or, to the sea, fleet Simois doth slide:
> And so shall Hesiod too, while vines do bear,
> Or crooked sickles crop the ripen'd ear.
> Callimachus, though in invention low,
> Shall still be sung, since he in art doth flow.
> No loss shall come to Sophocles' proud vein;
> With sun and moon, Aratus shall remain.
> While slaves be false, fathers hard, and bawds be whorish
> Whilst harlots flatter, shall Menander flourish.
> Ennius, though rude, and Accius's high-rear'd strain,
> A fresh applause in every age shall gain,
> Of Varro's name, what ear shall not be told,
> Of Jason's Argo and the fleece of gold?
> Then shall Lucretius' lofty numbers die,
> When earth and seas in fire and flame shall fry.
> Tityrus, Tillage, AEnee shall be read,
> Whilst Rome of all the conquered world is head!
> Till Cupid's fires be out, and his bow broken,
> Thy verses, neat Tibullus, shall be spoken.

Our Gallus shall be known from east to west;
So shall Lycoris, whom he now loves best.
The suffering plough-share or the flint may wear;
But heavenly Poesy no death can fear.
Kings shall give place to it, and kingly shows,
The banks o'er which gold-bearing Tagus flows.
Kneel hinds to trash: me let bright Phoebus swell
With cups full flowing from the Muses' well.
Frost-fearing myrtle shall impale my head,
And of sad lovers I be often read.
Envy the living, not the dead, doth bite!
For after death all men receive their right.
Then, when this body falls in funeral fire,
My name shall live, and my best part aspire.

Enter OVID *senior, followed by Luscus,*
Tucca, and Lupus.

Ovid se. Your name shall live, indeed, sir! you say true: but how infamously, how scorn'd and contemn'd in the eyes and ears of the best and gravest Romans, that you think not on; you never so much as dream of that. Are these the fruits of all my travail and expenses? Is this the scope and aim of thy studies? Are these the hopeful courses, wherewith I have so long flattered my expectation from thee? Verses! Poetry! Ovid, whom I thought to see the pleader, become Ovid the play-maker!

Ovid ju. No, sir.

Ovid se. Yes, sir; I hear of a tragedy of yours coming forth for the common players there, call'd Medea. By my household gods, if I come to the acting of it, I'll add one tragic part more than is yet expected to it: believe me, when I promise it. What! shall I have

my son a stager now? an enghle for players? a gull, a rook, a
shot-clog, to make suppers, and be laugh'd at? Publius, I will set
thee on the funeral pile first.

Ovid ju. Sir, I beseech you to have patience.

Lus. Nay, this 'tis to have your ears damn'd up to good counsel. I
did augur all this to him beforehand, without poring into an ox's
paunch for the matter, and yet he would not be scrupulous.

Tuc. How now, goodman slave! what, rowly-powly? all rivals, rascal?
Why, my master of worship, dost hear? are these thy best projects?
is this thy designs and thy discipline, to suffer knaves to be
competitors with commanders and gentlemen? Are we parallels, rascal,
are we parallels?

Ovid se. Sirrah, go get my horses ready. You'll still be prating.

Tuc. Do, you perpetual stinkard, do, go; talk to tapsters and
ostlers, you slave; they are in your element, go; here be the
emperor's captains, you raggamuffin rascal, and not your comrades.
                    [Exit Luscus.
Lup. Indeed. Marcus Ovid, these players are an idle generation, and
do much harm in a state, corrupt young gentry very much, I know it;
I have not been a tribune thus long and observed nothing: besides,
they will rob us, us, that are magistrates, of our respect, bring
us upon their stages, and make us ridiculous to the plebeians; they
will play you or me, the wisest men they can come by still, only to
bring us in contempt with the vulgar, and make us cheap.

Tur. Thou art in the right, my venerable cropshin, they will
indeed; the tongue of the oracle never twang'd truer. Your courtier
cannot kiss his mistress's slippers in quiet for them; nor your

white innocent gallant pawn his revelling suit to make his punk a
supper. An honest decayed commander cannot skelder, cheat, nor be
seen in a bawdy-house, but he shall be straight in one of their
wormwood comedies. They are grown licentious, the rogues;
libertines, flat libertines. They forget they are in the statute,
the rascals; they are blazon'd there; there they are trick'd, they
and their pedigrees; they need no other heralds, I wiss.

Ovid se. Methinks, if nothing else, yet this alone, the very
reading of the public edicts, should fright thee from commerce with
them, and give thee distaste enough of their actions. But this
betrays what a student you are, this argues your proficiency in the
law!

Ovid ju.
   They wrong me, sir, and do abuse you more,
   That blow your ears with these untrue reports.
   I am not known unto the open stage,
   Nor do I traffic in their theatres:
   Indeed, I do acknowledge, at request
   Of some near friends, and honourable Romans,
   I have begun a poem of that nature.

Ovid se. You have, sir, a poem! and where is it? That's the law you
study.

Ovid ju. Cornelius Gallus borrowed it to read.

Ovid se. Cornelius Gallus! there's another gallant too hath drunk
of the same poison, and Tibullus and Propertius. But these are
gentlemen of means and revenues now. Thou art a younger brother,
and hast nothing but they bare exhibition; which I protest shall be
bare indeed, if thou forsake not these unprofitable by-courses,

and that timely too. Name me a profest poet, that his poetry did ever afford him so much as a competency. Ay, your god of poets there, whom all of you admire and reverence so much, Homer, he whose worm-eaten statue must not be spewed against, but with hallow'd lips and groveling adoration, what was he? what was he?

Tuc. Marry, I'll tell thee, old swaggerer; he was a poor blind, rhyming rascal, that lived obscurely up and down in booths and tap-houses, and scarce ever made a good meal in his sleep, the whoreson hungry beggar.

Ovid se. He says well:--nay, I know this nettles you now; but answer me, is it not true? You'll tell me his name shall live; and that now being dead his works have eternised him, and made him divine: but could this divinity feed him while he lived? could his name feast him?

Tuc. Or purchase him a senator's revenue, could it?

Ovid se. Ay, or give him place in the commonwealth? worship, or attendants? make him be carried in his litter?

Tuc. Thou speakest sentences, old Bias.

Lup. All this the law will do, young sir, if you'll follow it.

Ovid se. If he be mine, he shall follow and observe what I will apt him to, or I profess here openly and utterly to disclaim him.

Ovid ju.
  Sir, let me crave you will forego these moods;
  I will be any thing, or study any thing;
  I'll prove the unfashion'd body of the law

> Pure elegance, and make her rugged'st strains
> Run smoothly as Propertius' elegies

Ovid se. Propertius' elegies? good!

Lup. Nay, you take him too quickly, Marcus

Ovid se. Why, he cannot speak, he cannot think out of poetry; he is bewitch'd with it.

Lup. Come, do not misprise him. Ovid se. Misprise! ay, marry, I would have him use some such words now; they have some touch, some taste of the law. He should make himself a style out of these, and let his Propertius' elegies go by.

Lup. Indeed, young Publius, he that will now hit the mark, must shoot through the law; we have no other planet reigns, and in that sphere you may sit and sing with angels. Why, the law makes a man happy, without respecting any other merit; a simple scholar, or none at all, may be a lawyer.

Tuc. He tells thee true, my noble neophyte; my little gram maticaster, he does: it shall never put thee to thy mathematics, metaphysics, philosophy, and I know not what supposed Suficiencies; if thou canst but have the patience to plod enough, talk, and make a noise enough, be impudent enough, and 'tis enough.

Lup. Three books will furnish you. Tuc. And the less art the better: besides, when it shall be in the power of thy chevril conscience, to do right or wrong at thy pleasure, my pretty Alcibiades.

Lup. Ay, and to have better men than himself, by many thousand degrees, to observe him, and stand bare.

Tuc. True, and he to carry himself proud and stately, and have the law on his side for't, old boy.

Ovid se. Well, the day grows old, gentlemen, and I must leave you. Publius, if thou wilt hold my favour, abandon these idle, fruitless studies, that so bewitched thee. Send Janus home his back face again, and look only forward to the law: intend that. I will I allow thee what shall suit thee in the rank of gentlemen, and maintain thy society with the best; and under these conditions I leave thee. My blessings light upon thee, if thou respect them; if not, mine eyes may drop for thee, but thine own heart will ache for itself; and so farewell! What, are my horses come?

Lus. Yes, sir, they are at the gate Without.

Ovid se. That's well.--Asinius Lupus, a word. Captain, I shall take my leave of you?

Tuc. No, my little old boy, dispatch with Cothurnus there: I'll attend thee, I--

Lus. To borrow some ten drachms: I know his project.
[Aside.
Ovid se. Sir, you shall make me beholding to you. Now, captain Tucca, what say you?

Tuc. Why, what should say, or what can I say, my flower O' the order? Should I say thou art rich, or that thou art honourable, or wise, or valiant, or learned, or liberal? why, thou art all these, and thou knowest it, my noble Lucullus, thou knowest it. Come, be not ashamed of thy virtues, old stump: honour's a good brooch to

wear in a man's hat at all times. Thou art the man of war's
Mecaenas, old boy. Why shouldst not thou be graced then by them, as
well as he is by his poets?
    [Enter PYRGUS and whispers TUCCA.
How now, my carrier, what news?

Lus. The boy has stayed within for his cue this half-hour.
    [Aside.
Tuc. Come, do not whisper to me, but speak it out: what; itis no
treason against the state I hope, is it?

Lus. Yes, against the state of my master's purse.
    [Aside, and exit.
Pyr. [aloud.] Sir, Agrippa desires you to forbear him till the next
week; his mules are not yet come up.

Tuc. His mules! now the bots, the spavin, and the glanders, and
some dozen diseases more, light on him and his mules! What, have
they the yellows, his mules, that they come no faster? or are
they foundered, ha? his mules have the staggers belike, have they?

Pyr. O no, sir;--then your tongue might be suspected for one of his
mules.
    [Aside.
Tuc He owes me almost a talent, and he thinks to bear it away with
his mules, does he? Sirrah, you nut cracker. Go your ways to him
again, and tell him I must have money, I: I cannot eat stones and
turfs, say. What, will he clem me and my followers? ask him an he
will clem me; do, go. He would have me fry my jerkin, would he?
Away, setter, away. Yet, stay, my little tumbler, this old boy
shall supply now. I will not trouble him, I cannot be importunate,
I; I cannot be impudent.

Pyr. Alas, sir, no; you are the most maidenly blushing creature upon the earth.
[Aside

Tuc. Dost thou hear, my little six and fifty, or thereabouts? thou art not to learn the humours and tricks of that old bald cheater, Time; thou hast not this chain for nothing. Men of worth have their chimeras, as well as other creatures; and they do see monsters sometimes, they do, they do, brave boy.

Pyr. Better cheap than he shall see you, I warrant him.
[Aside.

Tuc. Thou must let me have six-six drachma, I mean, old boy: thou shalt do it; I tell thee, old boy, thou shalt, and in private too,--dost thou see? --Go, walk off: [to the Boy]-There, there. Six is the sum. Thy son's a gallant spark and must not be put out of a sudden. Come hither, Callimachus; thy father tells me thou art too poetical, boy: thou must not be so; thou must leave them, young novice, thou must; they are a sort of poor starved rascals, that are ever wrap'd up in foul linen; and can boast of nothing but a lean visage, peering out of a seam-rent suit, the very emblems of beggary. No, dost hear, turn lawyer, thou shalt be my solicitor.---
'Tis right, old boy, is't?

Ovid Sr. You were best tell it, captain.

Tuc. No; fare thou well, mine honest horseman; and thou, old beaver. [To Lupus]-Pray thee, Roman, when thou comest to town, see me at my lodging, visit me sometimes? thou shalt be welcome. old boy. Do not balk me, good swaggerer. Jove keep thy chain from pawning; go thy ways, if thou lack money I'll lend thee some; I'll leave thee to thy horse now. Adieu. . .

Ovid Sr. Farewell, good captain.

Tuc. Boy, you can have but half a share now, boy
                              [Exit, followed by Pyrgus.
Ovid Sr. 'Tis a strange boldness that accompanies this fellow. Come.

Ovid ju. I'll give attendance on you to your horse, sir, please you.

Ovid se. No; keep your chamber, and fall to your studies; do so:
The gods of Rome bless thee!   [Exit with Lupus.

Ovid ju.
  And give me stomach to digest this law:
  That should have follow'd sure, had I been he.
  O, sacred Poesy, thou spirit of arts,
  The soul of science, and the queen of souls;
  What profane violence, almost sacrilege,
  Hath here been offered thy divinities!
  That thine own guiltless poverty should arm
  Prodigious ignorance to wound thee thus!
  For thence is all their force of argument,
  Drawn forth against thee; or, from the abuse
  Of thy great powers in adulterate brains:
  When, would men learn but to distinguish spirits
  And set true difference 'twixt those jaded wits
  That run a broken pace for common hire,
  And the high raptures of a happy muse,
  Borne on the wings of her immortal thought,
  That kicks at earth with a disdainful heel,
  And beats at heaven gates with her bright hoofs;
  They would not then, with such distorted faces,
  And desperate censures, stab at Poesy.
  They would admire bright knowledge, and their minds

Should ne'er descend on so unworthy objects
As gold, or titles; they would dread far more
To be thought ignorant, than be known poor.
The time was once, when wit drown'd wealth; but now,
Your only barbarism is t'have wit, and want.
No matter now in virtue who excels,
He that hath coin, hath all perfection else.

Tib. [within.] Ovid!

Ovid. Who's there? Come in.
                    Enter Tibullus.
Tib. Good morrow, lawyer.

Ovid. Good morrow, dear Tibullus; welcome: sit down.

Tib. Not I. What, so hard at it? Let's see, what's here? Numa in decimo nono. I Nay, I will see it

Ovid. Prithee away

Tib.
  If thrice in field a man vanquish his foe,
  'Tis after in his choice to serve or no.
  How, now, Ovid! Law cases in verse?

Ovid. In truth, I know not; they run from my pen unwittingly if they be verse. What's the news abroad?

Tib. Off with this. gown; I come to have thee walk.

Ovid. No, good Tibullus, I'm not now in case. Pray let me alone.

Tib. How! Not in case?
  Slight, thou'rt in too much case, by all this law.

Ovid.
  Troth, if I live, I will new dress the law
  In sprightly Poesy's habiliments.

Tib. The hell thou wilt! What! turn law into verse
Thy father has school'd thee, I see. Here, read that same;
There's subject for you; and, if I mistake not, A supersedeas
to your melancholy.

Ovid. How! subscribed Julia! O my life, my heaven!

Tib. Is the mood changed ?

Ovid.
  Music of wit! note for th' harmonious spheres!
  Celestial accents, how you ravish me!

Tib. What is it, Ovid?

Ovid. That I must meet my Julia, the princess Julia.

Tib. Where?

Ovid. Why, at---
  Heart, I've forgot; my passion so transports me.

Tib.
  I'll save your pains: it is at Albius' house,
  The jeweller's, where the fair Lycoris lies.

Ovid. Who? Cytheris, Cornelius Gallus' love?

Tib. Ay, he'll be there too, and my Plautia.

Ovid. And why not your Delia?

Tib. Yes, and your Corinna.

Ovid.
  True; but, my sweet Tibullus, keep that secret
  I would not, for all Rome, it should be thought
  I veil bright Julia underneath that name:
  Julia, the gem and jewel of my soul,
  That takes her honours from the golden sky,
  As beauty doth all lustre from her eye.
  The air respires the pure Elysian sweets
  In which she breathes, and from her looks descend
  The glories of the summer. Heaven she is,
  Praised in herself above all praise; and he
  Which hears her speak, would swear the tuneful orbs
  Turn'd in his zenith only.

Tib. Publius, thou'lt lose thyself.

Ovid.
  O, in no labyrinth can I safelier err,
  Than when I lose myself in praising her.
  Hence, law, and welcome Muses, though not rich,
  Yet are you pleasing: let's be reconciled,
  And new made one. Henceforth, I promise faith
  And all my serious hours to spend with you;
  With you, whose music striketh on my heart,
  And with bewitching tones steals forth my spirit,

In Julia's name; fair Julia: Julia's love
  Shall be a law, and that sweet law I'll study,
  The law and art of sacred Julia's love:
  All other objects will but abjects prove.

Tib. Come, we shall have thee as passionate as Propertius, anon.

Ovid. O, how does my Sextus?

Tib. Faith, full of sorrow for his Cynthia's death.

Ovid. What, still?

Tib.
  Still, and still more, his griefs do grow upon him
  As do his hours. Never did I know
  An understanding spirit so take to heart
  The common work of Fate.

Ovid.
  O, my Tibullus,
  Let us not blame him; for against such chances
  The heartiest strife of virtue is not proof.
  We may read constancy and fortitude.
  To other souls; but had ourselves been struck
  With the like planet, had our loves, like his,
  Been ravish'd from us by injurious death,
  And in the height and heat of our best days,
  It would have crack'd our sinews, shrunk our veins,
  And made our very heart-strings jar, like his.
  Come, let's go take him forth, and prove if mirth
  Or company will but abate his passion.

Tib. Content, and I implore the gods it may.
                              [Exeunt.

ACT II

SCENE I. A Room in ALBIUS'S House.
Enter ALBIUS and CRISPINUS.

Alb. Master Crispinus, you are welcome: pray use a stool, sir. Your cousin Cytheris will come down presently. We are so busy for the receiving of these courtiers here, that I can scarce be a minute with myself, for thinking of them: Pray you sit, sir; pray you sit, sir.

Crisp. I am very well, sir. Never trust me, but your are most delicately seated here, full of sweet delight and blandishment! an excellent air, an excellent air!

Alb. Ay, sir, 'tis a pretty air. These courtiers run in my mind still; I must look out. For Jupiter's sake, sit, sir; or please you walk into the garden? There's a garden on the back-side.

Crisp. I am most strenuously well, I thank you, sir.

Alb. Much good do you, sir.
              [Enter CHLOE, with two Maids.
Chloe. Come, bring those perfumes forward a little, and strew some roses and violets here: Fie! here be rooms savour the most

pitifully rank that ever I felt. I cry the gods mercy, [sees Albius] my husband's in the wind of us!

Alb. Why, this is good, excellent, excellent! well said, my sweet Chloe; trim up your house most obsequiously.

Chloe. For Vulcan's sake, breathe somewhere else; in troth you overcome our perfumes exceedingly; you are too predominant.

Alb. Hear but my opinion, sweet wife.

Chloe. A pin for your pinion! In sincerity, if you be thus fulsome to me in every thing, I'll be divorced. Gods my body! you know what you were before I married you; I was a gentlewoman born, I; I lost all my friends to be a citizen's wife, because I heard, indeed, they kept their wives as fine as ladies; and that we might rule our husbands like ladies, and do what we listed; do you think I would have married you else?

Alb. I acknowledge, sweet wife:--She speaks the best of any woman in Italy, and moves as mightily; which makes me, I had rather she should make bumps on my head, as big as my two fingers, than I would offend her--But, sweet wife--

Chloe. Yet again! Is it not grace enough for you, that I call you husband, and you call me wife; but you must still be poking me, against my will, to things?

Alb. But you know, wife. here are the greatest ladies, and gallantest gentlemen of Rome, to be entertained in our house now; and I would fain advise thee to entertain them in the best sort, i'faith, wife.

Chloe. In sincerity, did you ever hear a man talk so idly? You would seem to be master! you would have your spoke in my cart! you would advise me to entertain ladies and gentlemen! Because you can marshal your pack-needles, horse-combs, hobby-horses, and wall-candlesticks in your warehouse better than I, therefore you can tell how to entertain ladies and gentlefolks better than I?

Alb. O, my sweet wife, upbraid me not with that; gain savours sweetly from any thing; he that respects to get, must relish all commodities alike, and admit no difference between oade and frankincense, or the most precious balsamum and a tar-barrel.

Chloe. Marry, foh! you sell snuffers too, if you be remember'd; but I pray you let me buy them out of your hand; for, I tell you true, I take it highly in snuff, to learn how to entertain gentlefolks of you, at these years, i'faith. Alas, man, there was not a gentleman came to your house in your t'other wife's time, I hope! nor a lady, nor music, nor masques! Nor you nor your house were so much as spoken of, before I disbased myself, from my hood and my farthingal, to these bum-rowls and your whale-bone bodice.

Alb. Look here, my sweet wife; I am mum, my dear mummia, my balsamum, my spermaceti, and my very city of---She has the most best, true, feminine wit in Rome!

Cris. I have heard so, sir; and do most vehemently desire to participate the knowledge of her fair features.

Alb. Ah, peace; you shall hear more anon: be not seen yet, I pray you; not yet: observe.
                              [Exit.
Chloe. 'Sbody! give husbands the head a little more, and they'll be nothing but head shortly: What's he there?

1 Maid. I know not, forsooth.

2 Maid. Who would you speak with, sir?

Cris. I would speak with my cousin Cytheris.

2 Maid. He is one, forsooth, would speak with his cousin Cytheris.

Chloe. Is she your cousin, sir?

Cris. [coming forward.] Yes, in truth, forsooth, for fault of a better.

Chloe. She is a gentlewoman.

Cris. Or else she should not be my cousin, I assure you.

Chloe. Are you a gentleman born?

Cris. That I am, lady; you shall see mine arms, if it please you.

Chloe. No, your legs do sufficiently shew you are a gentleman born, sir; for a man borne upon little legs, is always a gentleman born.

Cris. Yet, I pray you, vouchsafe the sight of my arms, mistress; for I bear them about me, to have them seen: My name is Crispinus or Crispinas indeed; which is well expressed in my arms; a face crying in chief; and beneath it a bloody toe, between three thorns pungent.

Chloe. Then you are welcome, sir: now you are a gentleman born, I can find in my heart to welcome you; for I am a gentlewoman born too, and will bear my head high enough, though 'twere my fortune to marry a tradesman.

Cris. No doubt of that, sweet feature; your carriage shews it in any man's eye, that is carried upon you with judgment.

[Re-enter ALBIUS.

Alb. Dear wife, be not angry.

Chloe. Gods my passion!

Alb. Hear me but one thing; let not your maids set cushions in the parlour windows, nor in the dining-chamber windows; nor upon stools, in either of them, in any case; for 'tis tavern-like: but lay them one upon another, in some out-room or corner of the dining-chamber.

Chloe. Go, go; meddle with your bed-chamber only; or rather, with your bed in your chamber only; or rather with your wife in your bed only; or on my faith I'll not be pleased with you only.

Alb. Look here, my dear wife, entertain that gentleman kindly, I prithee--mum.

[Exit.

Chloe. Go, I need your instructions indeed! anger me no more, I advise you. Citi-sin, quotha! she's a wise gentlewoman, i'faith, will marry herself to the sin of the city.

Alb. [re-entering.] But this time, and no more, by heav'n, wife: hang no pictures in the hall, nor in the dining-chamber, in any case; But in the gallery only; for 'tis not courtly else, O' my word, wife.

Chloe. 'Sprecious, never have done!

Alb. Wife--

[Exit.

Chloe. Do I not bear a reasonable corrigible hand over him, , Crispinus?

Cris. By this hand, lady, you hold a most sweet hand over him.

Alb. [re-entering.] And then, for the great gilt andirons--

Chloe. Again! Would the andirons were in your great guts for me!

Alb. I do vanish, wife.

[Exit.

Chloe. How shall I do, master Crispinus? here will be all the bravest ladies in court presently to see your cousin Cytheris: O the gods! how might I behave myself now, as to entertain them most courtly?

Cris. Marry, lady, if you will entertain them most courtly, you must do thus: as soon as ever your maid or your man brings you word they are come, you must say, A pox on 'em ! what do they here? And yet, when they come, speak them as fair, and give them the kindest welcome in words that can be. . . .

Chloe. Is that the fashion of courtiers, Crispinus?

Cris. I assure you it is, lady; I have observed it.

Chloe. For your pox, sir, it is easily hit on; but it is not so easy to speak fair after, methinks.

Alb. [re-entering.] O, wife, the coaches are come, on my word; a number of coaches and courtiers.

Chloe. A pox on them! what do they here?

Alb. How now, wife! would'st thou not have them come?

Chloe. Come! Come, you are a fool, you.--He knows not the trick on't. Call Cytheris, I pray you: and, good master Crispinus, you can observe, you say; let me entreat you for all the ladies' behaviours, jewels, jests, and attires, that you marking, as well as I, we may put both our marks together, when they are gone, and confer of them.

Cris. I warrant you, sweet lady; let me alone to observe till I turn myself to nothing but observation.--
                        [Enter CYTHERIS.
Good morrow, cousin Cytheris.

Cyth. Welcome, kind cousin. What! are they come?

Alb. Ay, your friend Cornelius Gallus, Ovid, Tibullus, Propertius, with Julia, the emperor's daughter, and the lady Plautia, are 'lighted at the door; and with them Hermogenes Tigellius, the excellent musician.

Cyth. Come, let us go meet them, Chloe.

Chloe. Observe, Crispinus.

Crisp. At a hail's breadth, lady, I warrant you.

                [As they are going out, enter
                   CORNELIUS GALLUS, OVID, TIBULLUS,

PROPERTIUS, HERMOGENES, JULIA, and PLAUTIA.

Gal. Health to the lovely Chloe! you must pardon me, mistress, that I prefer this fair gentlewoman.

Cyth. I pardon and praise you for it, sir; and I beseech your excellence, receive her beauties into your knowledge and favour.

Jul. Cytheris, she hath favour and behaviour, that commands as much of me: and, sweet Chloe, know I do exceedingly love you, and that I will approve in any grace my father the emperor may shew you. Is this your husband?

Alb. For fault of a better, if it please your highness.

Chloe. Gods my life, how he shames me!

Cyth. Not a whit, Chloe, they all think you politic and witty; wise women choose not husbands for the eye, merit, or birth, but wealth and sovereignty.

Ovid. Sir, we all come to gratulate, for the good report of you.

Tib. And would be glad to deserve your love, sir.

Alb. My wife will answer you all, gentlemen; I'll come to you again presently.
[Exit.

Plau. You have chosen you a most fair companion here, Cytheris, and a very fair house.

Cyth. To both which, you and all my friends are very welcome, Plautia.

Chloe. With all my heart, I assure your ladyship.

Plau. Thanks, sweet mistress Chloe.

Jul. You must needs come to court, lady, i'faith, and there be sure your welcome shall be as great to us.

Ovid. She will deserve it, madam; I see, even in her looks, gentry, and general worthiness.

Tib. I have not seen a more certain character of an excellent disposition.

Alb. [re-entering.] Wife!

Chloe. O, they do so commend me here, the courtiers! what's the matter now?

Alb. For the banquet, sweet wife.

Chloe. Yes; and I must needs come to court, and be welcome, the princess says.
[Exit with Albius.
Gal. Ovid and Tibullus, you may be bold to welcome your mistress here.

Ovid. We find it so, sir.

Tib. And thank Cornelius Gallus.

Ovid. Nay, my sweet Sextus, in faith thou art not sociable.

Prop.
  In faith I am not, Publius; nor I cannot.
  Sick minds are like sick men that burn with fevers,
  Who when they drink, please but a present taste,
  And after bear a more impatient fit.
  Pray let me leave you; I offend you all,
  And myself most.

Gal. Stay, sweet Propertius.

Tib.
  You yield too much unto your griefs and fate,
  Which never hurts, but when we say it hurts us.

Prop.
  O peace, Tibullus; your philosophy
  Lends you too rough a hand to search my wounds.
  Speak they of griefs, that know to sigh and grieve:
  The free and unconstrained spirit feels
  No weight of my oppression.
                              [Exit.
Ovid.
  Worthy Roman!
  Methinks I taste his misery, and could
  Sit down, and chide at his malignant stars.

Jul. Methinks I love him, that he loves so truly.

Cyth. This is the perfect'st love, lives after death.

Gal. Such is the constant ground of virtue still.

Plau. It puts on an inseparable face.

[re-enter CHLOE.

Chloe. Have you mark'd every thing, Crispinus?

Cris. Every thing, I warrant you.

Chloe. What gentlemen are these? do you know them?

Cris. Ay, they are poets, lady.

Chloe. Poets! they did not talk of me since I went, did they?

Cris. O yes, and extolled your perfections to the heavens.

Chloe. Now in sincerity they be the finest kind of men that ever I knew: Poets! Could not one get the emperor to make my husband a poet, think you?

Cris. No, lady, 'tis love and beauty make poets: and since you like poets so well, your love and beauties shall make me a poet.

Chloe. What! shall they? and such a one as these?

Cris. Ay, and a better than these: I would be sorry else.

Chloe. And shall your looks change, and your hair change, and all, like these?

Cris. Why, a man may be a poet, and yet not change his hair, lady.

Chloe. Well, we shall see your cunning: yet, if you can change your hair, I pray do.
                [Re-enter Albius.
Alb. Ladies, and lordlings, there's a slight banquet stays within

for you; please you draw near, and accost it.

Jul. We thank you, good Albius: but when shall we see those excellent jewels you are commended to have?

Alb. At your ladyship's service.--I got that speech by seeing a play last day, and it did me some grace now: I see, 'tis good to collect sometimes; I'll frequent these plays more than I have done, now I come to be familiar with courtiers.　　　　[Aside.

Gal. Why, how now, Hermogenes? what ailest thou, trow?

Her, A little melancholy; let me alone, prithee.

Gal. Melancholy I how so?

Her. With riding: a plague on all coaches for me!

Chloe. Is that hard-favour'd gentleman a poet too, Cytheris?

Cyth. No, this is Hermogenes: as humorous as a poet, though: he is a musician.

Chloe. A musician! then he can sing.

Cyth. That he can, excellently; did you never hear him?

Chloe. O no: will he be entreated, think you?

Cyth. I know not.--Friend, mistress Chloe would fain hear Hermogenes sing: are you interested in him?

Gal. No doubt, his own humanity will command him so far, to the

satisfaction of so fair a beauty; but rather than fail, we'll all
be suitors to him.

Her. 'Cannot sing.

Gal. Prithee, Hermogenes.

Her. 'Cannot sing.

Gal. For honour of this gentlewoman, to whose house I know thou
mayest be ever welcome.

Chloe. That he shall, in truth, sir, if he can sing.

Ovid. What's that?

Gal. This gentlewoman is wooing Hermogenes for a song.

Ovid. A song! come, he shall not deny her. Hermogenes!

Her. 'Cannot sing.

Gal. No, the ladies must do it; he stays but to have their thanks
acknowledged as a debt to his cunning.

Jul. That shall not want; ourself will be the first shall promise
to pay him more than thanks, upon a favour so worthily vouchsafed.

Her. Thank you, madam; but 'will not sing.

Tib. Tut, the only way to win him, is to abstain from entreating
him.

Cris: Do you love singing, lady?

Chloe. O, passingly.

Cris. Entreat the ladies to entreat me to sing then, I beseech you.

Chloe. I beseech your grace, entreat this gentleman to sing.

Jul. That we will, Chloe; can he sing excellently?

Chloe. I think so, madam; for he entreated me to entreat you to entreat him to sing.

Cris. Heaven and earth! would you tell that?

Jul. Good, sir, let's entreat you to use your voice.

Cris. Alas, madam, I cannot, in truth.

Fla. The gentleman is modest: I warrant you he sings excellently.

Ovid. Hermogenes, clear your throat: I see by him, here's a gentleman will worthily challenge you.

Cris. Not I, sir, I'll challenge no man.

Tib. That's your modesty, sir; but we, out of an assurance of your excellency, challenge him in your behalf.

Cris. I thank you, gentlemen, I'll do my best.

Her. Let that best be good, sir, you were best.

Gal. O, this contention is excellent! What is't you sing, sir?

Cris. If I freely may discover, sir; I'll sing that.

Ovid. One of your own compositions, Hermogenes. He offers you vantage enough.

Cris. Nay, truly, gentlemen, I'll challenge no man.--I can sing but one staff of the ditty neither.

Gal. The better: Hermogenes himself will be entreated to sing the other.

    CRISPINUS sings.

> If I freely may discover
> What would please me in my lover,
> I would have her fair and witty,
> Savouring more of court than city;
> A little proud, but full of pity:
> Light and humorous in her toying,
> Oft building hopes, and soon destroying,
> Long, but sweet in the enjoying;
> Neither too easy nor too hard:
> All extremes I would have barr'd.

Gal. Believe me, sir, you sing most excellently.

Ovid. If there were a praise above excellence, the gentleman highly deserves it.

Her. Sir, all this doth not yet make me envy you; for I know I sing better than you.

Tib. Attend Hermogenes, now.

             HERMOGENES, accompanied.

>She should be allow'd her passions,
>So they were but used as fashions;
>Sometimes froward, and then frowning,
>Sometimes sickish and then swowning,
>Every fit with change still crowning.
>Purely jealous I would have her,
>Then only constant when I crave her:
>'Tis a virtue should not save her.
>Thus, nor her delicates would cloy me,
>Neither her peevishness annoy me.

Jill. Nay, Hermogenes, your merit hath long since been 'both known and admired of us.

Her. You shall hear me sing another. Now will I begin.

Gal. We shall do this gentleman's banquet too much wrong, that stays for us, ladies.

Jul. 'Tis true; and well thought on, Cornelius Gallus.

Her. Why, 'tis but a short air, 'twill be done presently, pray stay: strike, music.

Ovid. No, good Hermogenes; we'll end this difference within.

Jul. 'Tis the common disease of all your musicians, that they know no mean. to be entreated either to begin or end.

Alb. Please you lead the way, gentles.

All. Thanks, good Albius.
> [Exeunt all but Albius.

Alb. O, what a charm of thanks was here put upon me! O Jove, what a setting forth it is to a man to have many courtiers come to his house! Sweetly was it said of a good old housekeeper, I had, rather want meat, than want guests, especially, if they be courtly guests. For, never trust me, if one of their good legs made in a house be not worth all the good cheer a man can make them. He that would have fine guests, let him have a fine wife! he that would have a fine wife, let him come to me.
> [Re-enter CRISPINUS.

Cris. By your kind leave, master Albius.

Alb. What, you are not gone, master Crispinus?

Cris. Yes, faith, I have a design draws me hence: pray, sir, fashion me an excuse to the ladies.

Alb. Will you not stay and see the jewels, sir? I pray you stay.

Cris. Not for a million, sir, now. Let it suffice, I must relinquish; and so, in a word, please you to expiate this compliment.

Alb. Mum.
> [Exit.

Cris. I'll presently go and enghle some broker for a poet's gown, and bespeak a garland: and then, jeweller, look to your best jewel, i'faith.
> [Exit.

ACT III

SCENE I.-The Via Sacra (or Holy Street).

Enter HORACE, CRISPINUS following.

Hor. Umph! yes, I will begin an ode so; and it shall be to Mecaenas.

Cris. 'Slid, yonder's Horace! they say he's an excellent poet: Mecaenas loves him. I'll fall into his acquaintance, if I can; I think he be composing as he goes in the street! ha! 'tis a good humour, if he be: I'll compose too.

Hor.
  Swell me a bowl with lus'y wine,
  Till I may see the plump Lyoeus swim
        Above the brim:
  I drink as I would write,
  In flowing measure fill'd with flame and sprite.

Cris. Sweet Horace, Minerva and the Muses stand auspicious to thy designs! How farest thou, sweet man? frolic? rich? gallant? ha!

Hor. Not greatly gallant, Sir; like my fortunes, well: I am bold to take my leave, Sir; you'll nought else, Sir, would you?

Cris. Troth, no, but I could wish thou didst know us, Horace; we are a scholar, I assure thee.

Hor. A scholar, Sir! I shall be covetous of your fair knowledge.

Cris. Gramercy, good Horace. Nay, we are new turn'd poet too, which is more; and a satirist too, which is more than that: I write just in thy vein, I. I am for your odes, or your sermons, or any thing indeed; we are a gentleman besides; our name is Rufus Laberius Crispinus; we are a pretty Stoic too.

Hor. To the proportion of your beard, I think it, sir.

Cris. By Phoebus, here's a most neat, fine street, is't not? I protest to thee, I am enamoured of this street now, more than of half the streets of Rome again; 'tis so polite and terse! there's the front of a building now! I study architecture too: if ever I should build, I'd have a house just of that prospective.

Hor. Doubtless, this gallant's tongue has a good turn, when he sleeps.   [Aside.

Cris. I do make verses, when I come in such a street as this: O, your city ladies, you shall have them sit in every shop like the Muses--offering you the Castalian dews, and the Thespian liquors, to as many as have but the sweet grace and audacity to sip of their lips. Did you never hear any of my verses?

Bor. No, sir;---but I am in some fear I must now.   [Aside.

Cris. I'll tell thee some, if I can but recover them, I composed even now of a dressing I saw a jeweller's wife wear, who indeed was a jewel herself: I prefer that kind of tire now; what's thy opinion, Horace?

Hor. With your silver bodkin, it does well, sir.

Cris. I cannot tell; but it stirs me more than all your court-curls, or your spangles, or your tricks: I affect not these high gable-ends, these Tuscan tops, nor your coronets, nor your arches, nor your pyramids; give me a fine, sweet-little delicate dressing with a bodkin, as you say; and a mushroom for all your other ornatures!

Hor. Is it not possible to make an escape from him? [Aside.

Cris. I have remitted my verses all this while; I think I have forgot them.

Hor. Here's he could wish you had else. [Aside.

Chris. Pray Jove I can entreat them of my memory!

Hor. You put your memory to too much trouble, sir.

Cris. No, sweet Horace, we must not have thee think so.

Hor.
  I cry you mercy; then they are my ears
  That must be tortured: well, you must have patience, ears.

Cris. Pray thee, Horace, observe.

Hor. Yes, sir; your satin sleeve begins to fret at the rug that is underneath it, I do observe: and your ample velvet bases are not without evident stains of a hot disposition naturally.

Cris. O--I'll dye them into another colour, at pleasure: How many yards of velvet dost thou think they contain?

Hor.
  'Heart! I have put him now in a fresh way
  To vex me more:---faith, sir, your mercer's book
  Will tell you With more patience than I can:---
  For I am crost, and so's not that, I think.

Cris.
  'Slight, these verses have lost me again!
  I shall not invite them to mind, now.

Hor.
  Rack not your thoughts, good sir; rather defer it
  To a new time; I'll meet you at your lodging,
  Or where you please: 'till then, Jove keep you, sir!

Cris. Nay, gentle Horace, stay; I have it now.

Hor.
  Yes, sir. Apollo, Hermes, Jupiter,
  Look down upon me.   [Aside.

Cris.
  Rich was thy hap; sweet dainty cap,
      There to be placed;
  Where thy smooth black, sleek white may smack,
      And both be graced.

White is there usurp'd for her brow; her forehead: and then sleek, as the parallel to smooth, that went before. A kind of paranomasie, or agnomination: do you conceive, sir?

Hor. Excellent. Troth, sir, I must be abrupt, and leave you.

Cris. Why, what haste hast thou? prithee, stay a little; thou shalt not go yet, by Phoebus.

Hor. I shall not! what remedy? fie, how I sweat with suffering!

Cris. And then

Hor. Pray, sir, give me leave to wipe my face a little.

Cris. Yes, do, good Horace.

Hor.
  Thank you, sir.
  Death! I must crave his leave to p--, anon; .
  Or that I may go hence with half my teeth:
  I am in some such fear. This tyranny
  Is strange, to take mine ears up by commission,
  (Whether I will or no,) and make them stalls
  To his lewd solecisms, and worded trash.
  Happy thou, bold Bolanus, now I say;
  Whose freedom, and impatience of this fellow,
  Would, long ere this, have call'd him fool, and fool,
  And rank and tedious fool! and have flung jests
  As hard as stones, till thou hadst pelted him
  Out of the place; whilst my tame modesty
  Suffers my wit be made a solemn ass,
  To bear his fopperies   [Aside.

Cris. Horace, thou art miserably affected to be gone, I see. But--prithee let's prove to enjoy thee a while. Thou hast no business, I assure me. Whither is thy journey directed, ha?

Hor. Sir, I am going to visit a friend that's sick.

Cris A friend! what is he; do not I know him?

Hor. No, sir, you do not know him; and 'tis not the worse for him.

Cris. What's his name 1 where is he lodged?

Hor. Where I shall be fearful to draw you out of your way, sir; a great way hence; pray, sir, let's part.

Cris. Nay, but where is't? I prithee say. ;

Hor. On the far side of all Tyber yonder, by Caesar's gardens.

Cris. O, that's my course directly; I am for you. Come, go; why stand'st thou?

Hor. Yes, sir: marry, the plague is in that part of the city; I had almost forgot to tell you, sir.

Cris. Foh! it is no matter, I fear no pestilence; I have not offended Phoebus.

Hor.
  I have, it seems, or else this heavy scourge
  Could ne'er have lighted on me.

Cris. Come along. Hor. I am to go down some half mile this way, sir, first, to speak with his physician; and from thence to his apothecary, where I shall stay the mixing of divers drugs.

Cris. Why, it's all one, I have nothing to do, and I love not to be idle; I'll bear thee company. How call'st thou the apothecary?

Hor.
  O that I knew a name would fright him now!---
  Sir, Rhadamanthus, Rhadamanthus, sir.
  There's one so called, is a just judge in hell,
  And doth inflict strange vengeance on all those
  That here on earth torment poor patient spirits.

Cris. He dwells at the Three Furies, by Janus's temple.

Hor. Your pothecary does, sir.

Cris. Heart, I owe him money for sweetmeats, and he has laid to arrest me, I hear: but

Hor: Sir, I have made a most solemn vow, I will never bail any man.

Oris. Well then, I'll swear, and speak him fair, if the worst come. But his name is Minos, not Rhadamanthus, Horace.

Hor. That may be, sir, I but guess'd at his name by his sign. But your Minos is a judge too, sir.

Cris I protest to thee, Horace, (do but taste me once,) if I do know myself, and mine own virtues truly, thou wilt not make that esteem of Varius, or Virgil, or Tibullus, or any of 'em indeed, as now in thy ignorance thou dost; which I am content to forgive: I would fain see which of these could pen more verses in a day, or with more facility, than I; or that could court his mistress, kiss her hand, make better sport with her fan or her dog

Hor. I cannot bail you yet, sir.

Cris. Or that could move his body more gracefully, or dance better; you should see me, were it not in the street

Hor. Nor yet.

Cris. Why, I have been a reveller, and at my cloth of silver suit and my long stocking, in my time, and will be again

Hor. If you may be trusted, sir.

Cris. And then, for my singing, Hermogenes himself envies me, that is your only master of music you have in Rome.

Hor. Is your mother living, sir?

Cris. Ay! convert thy thoughts to somewhat else, I pray thee.

Hor. You have much of the mother in you, sir: Your father is dead?

Cris. Ay, I thank Jove, and my grandfather too, and all my kinsfolks, and well composed in their urns.

Hor.
  The more their happiness, that rest in peace,
  Free from the abundant torture of thy tongue:
  Would I were with them too!

Cris. What's that, Horace?

Hor.
  I now remember me, sir, of a sad fate
  A cunning woman, one Sabella, sung,
  When in her urn she cast my destiny,
  I being but a child.

Cris. What was it, I pray thee?

Hor.
  She told me I should surely never perish
  By famine, poison, or the enemy's sword;
  The hectic fever, cough, or pleurisy,
  Should never hurt me, nor the tardy gout:
  But in my time, I should be once surprised
  By a strong tedious talker, that should vex
  And almost bring me to consumption:
  Therefore, if I were wise, she warn'd me shun
  All such long-winded monsters as my bane;
  For if I could but 'scape that one discourser,
  I might no doubt prove an old aged man.--
  By your leave, Sir.   [Going.

Cris. Tut, tut; abandon this idle humour, 'tis nothing but melancholy. 'Fore Jove, now I think on't, I am to appear in court here, to answer to one that has me in suit: sweet Horace, go with me, this is my hour; if I neglect it, the law proceeds against me. Thou art familiar with these things; prithee, if thou lov'st me, go.

Hor.
  Now, let me die, sir, if I know your laws,

Or have the power to stand still half so long
In their loud courts, as while a case is argued.
Besides, you know, sir, where I am to go.
And the necessity---

Cris. 'Tis true.

Hor. I hope the hour of my release be come: he will, upon this consideration, discharge me, sure.

Cris. Troth, I am doubtful what I may best do, whether to leave thee or my affairs, Horace.

Hor. O Jupiter! me, sir, me, by any means; I beseech you, me, sir.

Cris. No, faith, I'll venture those now; thou shalt see I love thee--some, Horace.

Hor. Nay, then I am desperate: I follow you, sir. 'Tis hard contending with a man that overcomes thus.

Cris. And how deals Mecaenas with thee? liberally, ha? is he open handed? bountiful?

Hor. He's still himself, sir.

Cris. Troth, Horace, thou art exceeding happy in thy friends and acquaintance; they are all most choice spirits, and of the first rank of Romans: I do not know that poet, I protest, has used his fortune more prosperously than thou hast. If thou wouldst bring me known to Mecaenas, I should second thy desert well; thou shouldst find a good sure assistant of me, one that would speak all good of thee in thy absence, and be content with the next place, not envying thy reputation with thy patron. Let me not live, but I think thou and I, in a small time, should lift them all out of favour, both Virgil, Varius, and the best of them, and enjoy him wholly to ourselves.

Hor.
  Gods, you do know it, I can hold no longer;
  This brize has prick'd my patience. Sir, your silkness
  Clearly mistakes Mecaenas and his house,
  To think there breathes a spirit beneath his roof,
  Subject unto those poor affections
  Of undermining envy and detraction,
  Moods only proper to base grovelling minds.
  That place is not in Rome, I dare affirm,
  More pure or free from such low common evils.
  There's no man griev'd, that this is thought more rich,
  Or this more learned; each man hath his place,
  And to his merit his reward of grace,
  Which, with a mutual love, they all embrace.

Cris. You report a wonder: 'tis scarce credible, this.

Hor. l am no torturer to enforce you to believe it; but it is so

Cris. Why, this inflames me with a more ardent desire to be his, than before; but I doubt I shall find the entrance to his familiarity somewhat more than difficult, Horace.

Hor. Tut, you'll conquer him, as you have done me; there's no standing out against you, sir, I see that: either your importunity, or the intimation of your good parts, or

Cris. Nay, I'll bribe his porter, and the grooms of his chamber;

make his doors open to me that way first, and then I'll observe my times. Say he should extrude me his house to-day, shall I therefore desist, or let fall my suit to-morrow? No; I'll attend him, follow him, meet him in the street, the highways, run by his coach, never leave him. What! man hath nothing given him in this life without much labour

Hor.
  And impudence.
  Archer of heaven, Phoebus, take thy bow,
  And with a full-drawn shaft nail to the earth
  This Python, that I may yet run hence and live:
  Or, brawny Hercules, do thou come down,
  And, tho' thou mak'st it up thy thirteenth labour,
  Rescue me from this hydra of discourse here.
              [Enter FUSCUS ARISTIUS.

Ari. Horace, well met.

Hor.
  O welcome, my reliever;
  Aristius, as thou lov'st me, ransom me.

Ari. What ail'st thou, man?

Hor.
  'Death, I am seized on here
  By a land remora; I cannot stir,
  Nor move, but as he pleases.

Cris. Wilt thou go, Horace?

Hor.
  Heart! he cleaves to me like Alcides' shirt,

Tearing my flesh and sinews: O, I've been vex'd
And tortured with him beyond forty fevers.
For Jove's sake, find some means to take me from him.

Ari. Yes, I will;--but I'll go first and tell Mecaenas.   [Aside.

Cris. Come, shall we go?

Ari. The jest will make his eyes run, i'faith.   [Aside.

Hor. Nay, Aristius!

Ari. Farewell, Horace.   [Going.

Hor. 'Death! will he leave me? Fuscus Aristius! do you hear? Gods of Rome! You said you had somewhat to say to me in private.

Ari. Ay, but I see you are now employed with that gentleman; 'twere offence to trouble you; I'll take some fitter opportunity: farewell.   [Exit.

Hor.
  Mischief and torment! O my soul and heart,
  How are you cramp'd with anguish! Death itself
  Brings not the like convulsions, O, this day!
  That ever I should view thy tedious face.---

Cris. Horace, what passion, what humour is this?

Hor.
  Away, good prodigy, afflict me not.
  A friend, and mock me thus! Never was man
  So left under the axe.---

[Enter Minos with two Lictors.

How now?

Min. That's he in the embroidered hat, there, with the ash-colour'd feather: his name is Laberius Crispinus.

Lict. Laberius Crispinus, I arrest you in the emperor's name.

Cris. Me, sir! do you arrest me?

Lice. Ay, sir, at the suit of master Minos the apothecary.
[Exit hastily.
Hor. Thanks, great Apollo, I will not slip thy favour offered me in my escape, for my fortunes.

Cris. Master Minos! I know no master

Minos. Where's Horace? Horace! Horace!

Min. Sir, do not you know me?

Cris. O yes, I know you, master Minos; cry you mercy. But Horace? God's me, is he gone?

Min. Ay, and so would you too, if you knew how.--Officer, look to him.

Cris. Do you hear, master Minos? pray let us be used like a man of our own fashion. By Janus and Jupiter, I meant to have paid you next week every drachm. Seek not to eclipse my reputation thus vulgarly.

Min. Sir, your oaths cannot serve you; you know I have forborne you long.

Cris. I am conscious of it, sir. Nay, I beseech you, gentlemen, do not exhale me thus, remember 'tis but for sweetmeats--

Lict. Sweet meat must have sour sauce, sir. Come along.

Cris. Sweet master Minos, I am forfeited to eternal disgrace, if you do not commiserate. Good officer, be not so officious.
      Enter TUCCA and Pyrgi.
Tuc. Why, how now, my good brace of bloodhounds, whither do you drag the gentleman? You mongrels, you curs, you ban-dogs! we are captain Tucca that talk to you, you inhuman pilchers.

Min. Sir, he is their prisoner.

Tuc. Their pestilence! What are you, sir?

Min. A citizen of Rome, sir.

Tuc. Then you are not far distant from a fool, sir.

Min. A pothecary, sir.

Tuc. I knew thou wast not a physician: foh! out of my nostrils, thou stink'st of lotium and the syringe; away, quack-salver!-- Follower, my sword.
         [Aside.
1 Pyr. Here, noble leader; you'll do no harm with it, I'll trust you.

Tuc. Do you hear, you goodman, slave? Hook, ram, rogue, catchpole,

loose the gentleman, or by my velvet arms--
            [*Strikes up his heels, and seizes his sword.*
Lict. What will you do, sir?

Tuc. Kiss thy hand, my honourable active varlet, and embrace thee thus.

1 Pyr. O patient metamorphosis!

Tuc. My sword, my tall rascal.

Lict. Nay, soft, sir; some wiser than some.

Tuc. What! and a wit too? By Pluto, thou must be cherish'd, slave; here's three drachms for thee; hold.

2 Pyr. There's half his lendings gone.

Tuc. Give me.

Lict. No, sir, your first word shall stand; I'll hold all.

Tuc. Nay, but rogue--

Lict. You would make a rescue of our prisoner, sir, you.

Tuc. I a rescue! A way, inhuman varlet. Come, come, I never relish above one jest at most; do not disgust me, Sirrah; do not, rogue! I tell thee, rogue, do not.

Lict. How, sir! rogue?

Tuc. Ay; why, thou art not angry, rascal, art thou?

Lict. I cannot tell, sir; I am little better upon these terms.

Tuc. Ha, gods and fiends! why, dost hear, rogue, thou? give me thy hand; I say unto thee, thy hand, rogue. What, dost not thou know me? not me, rogue? not captain Tucca, rogue?

Min. Come, pray surrender the gentleman his sword, officer; we'll have no fighting here.

Tuc. What's thy name?

Min. Minos, an't please you.

Tuc. Minos! Come hither, Minos; thou art a wise fellow, it seems; let me talk with thee.

Cris. Was ever wretch so wretched as unfortunate I!

Tuc. Thou art one of the centumviri, old boy, art not?

Min. No indeed, master captain.

Tuc. Go to, thou shalt be then; I'll have thee one,

Minos. Take my sword from these rascals, dost thou see! go, do it; I cannot attempt with patience. What does this gentleman owe thee, little Minos?

Min. Fourscore sesterties, sir.

Tuc. What, no more! Come, thou shalt release him.

Minos: what, I'll be his bail, thou shalt take my word, old boy, and cashier these furies: thou shalt do't, I say, thou shalt, little Minos, thou shalt.

Cris. Yes; and as I am a gentleman and a reveller, I'll make a piece of poetry, and absolve all, within these five days.

Tuc. Come, Minos is not to learn how to use a gentleman of quality, I know.--My sword: If he pay thee not, I will, and I must, old boy. Thou shalt be my pothecary too. Hast good eringos, Minos.

Min. The best in Rome, sir.

Tuc. Go to, then--Vermin, know the house.

1 Pyr. I warrant you, colonel.

Tuc. For this gentleman, Minos--

Min. I'll take your word, captain.

Tuc. Thou hast it. My sword.

Min. Yes, sir: But you must discharge the arrest, master Crispinus.

Tuc. How, Minos! Look in the gentleman's face, and but read his silence. Pay, pay; 'tis honour, Minos.

Cris. By Jove, sweet captain, you do most infinitely endear and oblige me to you.

Tuc. Tut, I cannot compliment, by Mars; but, Jupiter love me, as I love good words and good clothes, and there's an end. Thou shalt give my boy that girdle and hangers, when thou hast worn them a little more.

Cris. O Jupiter! captain, he shall have them now, presently:--
Please you to be acceptive, young gentleman.

1 Pyr. Yes, sir, fear not; I shall accept; I have a pretty foolish humour of taking, if you knew all.   [Aside.

Tuc. Not now, you shall not take, boy.

Cris. By my truth and earnest, but he shall, captain, by your leave.

Tuc. Nay, an he swear by his truth and earnest, take it, boy: do not make a gentleman forsworn.

Lict. Well, sir, there's your sword; but thank master Minos; you had not carried it as you do else.

Tuc. Minos is just, and you are knaves, and

Lict. What say you, sir?

Tuc. Pass on, my good scoundrel, pass on, I honour thee: [Exeunt Lictors.] But that I hate to have action with such base rogues as these, you should have seen me unrip their noses now, and have sent them to the next barber's to stitching; for do you see---I am a man of humour, and I do love the varlets, the honest varlets, they have wit and valour, and are indeed good profitable,--errant rogues, as any live in an empire. Dost thou hear, poetaster? [To Crispinus.] Second me. Stand up, Minos, close, gather, yet, so! Sir, (thou shalt have a quarter-share, be resolute) you shall, at my request,

take Minos by the hand here, little Minos, I will have it so; all
friends, and a health; be not inexorable. And thou shalt impart the
wine, old boy, thou shalt do it, little Minos, thou shalt; make us
pay it in our physic. What! we must live, and honour the gods
sometimes; now Bacchus, now Comus, now Priapus; every god a little.
[Histrio passes by.] What's he that stalks by there, boy, Pyrgus?
You were best let him pass, Sirrah; do, ferret, let him pass, do

2 Pyr. 'Tis a player, sir.

Tuc. A player! call him, call the lousy slave hither; what, will he
sail by and not once strike, or vail to a man of war? ha!-Do you
hear, you player, rogue, stalker, come back here!
                    [Enter Histrio.
No respect to men of worship, you slave! what, you are proud, you
rascal, are you proud, ha? you grow rich, do you, and purchase,
you twopenny tear-mouth? you have FORTUNE, and the good year on
your side, you stinkard, you have, you have!

Hist. Nay, 'sweet captain, be confined to some reason; I protest I
saw you not, sir.

Tuc. You did not? where was your sight, OEdipus? you walk with
hare's eyes, do you? I'll have them glazed, rogue; an you say the
word, they shall be glazed for you: come we must have you turn
fiddler again, slave, get a base viol at your back, and march in a
tawny coat, with one sleeve, to Goose-fair; then you'll know us,
you'll see us then, you will, gulch, you will. Then, Will't please
your worship to have any music, captain?

Hist. Nay, good captain.

Tuc. What, do you laugh, Howleglas! death, you perstemptuous varlet, I am none of your fellows; I have commanded a hundred and fifty such rogues, I,

2 Pyr. Ay, and most of that hundred and fifty have been leaders of a legion. [Aside.

Hist. If I have exhibited wrong, I'll tender satisfaction, captain.

Tuc. Say'st thou so, honest vermin! Give me thy hand; thou shalt make us a supper one of these nights.

Hist. When you please, by Jove, captain, most willingly. us. Dost thou swear! To-morrow then; say and hold, slave. There are some of you players honest gentlemen-like scoundrels, and suspected to have some wit, as well as your poets, both at drinking and breaking of jests, and are companions for gallants. A man may skelder ye, now and then, of half a dozen shillings, or so. Dost thou not know that Pantalabus there?

Hist. No, I assure you, captain.

Tuc. Go; and be acquainted with him then; he is a gentleman, parcel poet, you slave; his father was a man of worship, I tell thee. Go, he pens high, lofty, in a new stalking strain, bigger than half the rhymers in the town again; he was born to fill thy mouth, Minotaurus, he was, he will teach thee to tear and rand. Rascal, to him, cherish his muse, go; thou hast forty-forty shillings, I mean, stinkard; give him in earnest, do, he shall write for thee, slave! If he pen for thee once, thou shalt not need to travel with thy pumps full of gravel any more, after a blind jade and a hamper, and stalk upon boards and barrel heads to an old crack'd trumpet.

Hist. Troth, I think I have not so much about me, captain.

Tuc. It's no matter; give him what thou hast, stiff-toe, I'll give my word for the rest; though it lack a shilling or two, it skills not: go, thou art an honest shifter; I'll have the statute repeal'd for thee.--Minos, I must tell thee, Minos, thou hast dejected yon gentleman's spirit exceedingly; dost observe, dost note, little Minos?

Min. Yes, sir.

Tuc. Go to then, raise, recover, do; suffer him not to droop in prospect of a player, a rogue, a stager: put twenty into his hand--twenty sesterces I mean,--and let nobody see; go, do it--the work shall commend itself; ye Minos, I'll pay.

Min. Yes, forsooth, captain.

2 Pyr. Do not we serve a notable shark?   [Aside.

Tuc. And what new matters have you now afoot, sirrah, ha? I would fain come with my cockatrice one day, and see a play, if I knew when there were a good bawdy one; but they say you have nothing but HUMOURS, REVELS, and SATIRES, that gird and f--t at the time, you slave.

Hist. No, I assure you, captain, not we. They are on the other side of Tyber: we have as much ribaldry in our plays as can be, as you would wish, captain: all the sinners in the suburbs come and applaud our action daily.

Tuc. I hear you'll bring me o' the stage there; you'll play me, they say; I shall be presented by a sort of copper-laced scoundrels of you: life of Pluto! an you stage me, stinkard, your mansions shall sweat for't, your tabernacles, varlets, your Globes, and your

Triumphs.

Hist. Not we, by Phoebus, captain; do not do us imputation without desert.

Tuc. I will not, my good twopenny rascal; reach me thy neuf. Dost hear? what wilt thou give me a week for my brace of beagles here, my little point-trussers? you shall have them act among ye.--I Sirrah, you, pronounce.--Thou shalt hear him speak in King Darius' doleful strain.

1 Pyr.
  O doleful days! O direful deadly dump!
  O wicked world, and worldly wickedness!
  How can I hold my fist from crying, thump,
  In rue of this right rascal wretchedness!

Tuc. In an amorous vein now, sirrah: peace!

1 Pyr.
  O, she is wilder, and more hard, withal,
  Than beast, or bird, or tree, or stony wall.
  Yet might she love me, to uprear her state:
  Ay, but perhaps she hopes some nobler mate.
  Yet might she love me, to content her fire:
  Ay, but her reason masters her desire.
  Yet might she love me as her beauty's thrall:
  Ay, but I fear she cannot love at all.

Tuc. Now, the horrible, fierce soldier, you, sirrah.

2 Pyr.
  What! will I brave thee? ay, and beard thee too;
  A Roman spirit scorns to bear a brain
  So full of base pusillanimity.

Hist. Excellent!

Tuc. Nay, thou shalt see that shall ravish thee anon; prick up thine ears, stinkard.--The ghost, boys!

1 Pyr. Vindicate!

2 Pyr. Timoria!

1 Pyr. Vindicta!

2 Pyr. Timoria!

1 Pyr. Veni!

2 Pyr. Veni!

Tuc. Now thunder, sirrah, you, the rumbling player.

2 Pyr. Ay, but somebody must cry, Murder! then, in a small voice.

Tuc. Your fellow-sharer there shall do't:

Cry, sirrah, cry.

1 Pyr. Murder, murder!

2 Pyr. Who calls out murder? lady, was it you?

Hist. O, admirable good, I protest.

Tuc. Sirrah, boy, brace your drum a little straiter, and do the t'other fellow there, he in the--what sha' call him--and yet stay too.

2 Pyr.
  Nay, an thou dalliest, then I am thy foe,
  And fear shall force what friendship cannot win;
  Thy death shall bury what thy life conceals.
  Villain! thou diest for more respecting her---

1 Pyr. O stay, my lord.

2 Pyr.
  Than me:
  Yet speak the truth, and I will guerdon thee;
  But if thou dally once again, thou diest.

Tuc. Enough of this, boy.

2 Pyr.
  Why, then lament therefore: d--n'd be thy guts
  Unto king Pluto's Hell, and princely Erebus;
  For sparrows must have food---

Hist. Pray, sweet captain, let one of them do a little of a lady.

Tuc. O! he will make thee eternally enamour'd of him, there: do, sirrah, do; 'twill allay your fellow's fury a little.

1 Pyr.
  Master, mock on; the scorn thou givest me,

Pray Jove some lady may return on thee.

2 Pyr. Now you shall see me do the Moor: master, lend me your scarf a little.

Tuc. Here, 'tis at thy service, boy.

2 Pyr. You, master Minos, hark hither a little
               [Exit with Minos, to make himself ready.
Tuc. How dost like him? art not rapt, art not tickled now? dost not applaud, rascal? dost not applaud?

Hist. Yes: what will you ask for them a week, captain?

Tuc. No, you mangonising slave, I will not part from them; you'll sell them for enghles, you: let's have good cheer tomorrow night at supper, stalker, and then we'll talk; good capon and plover, do you hear, sirrah? and do not bring your eating player with you there; I cannot away with him: he will eat a leg of mutton while I am in my porridge, the lean Polyphagus, his belly is like Barathrum; he looks like a midwife in man's apparel, the slave: nor the villanous out-of-tune fiddler, AEnobarbus, bring not him. What hast thou there? six and thirty, ha?

Hist. No, here's all I have, captain, some five and twenty: pray, sir, will you present and accommodate it unto the gentleman? for mine own part, I am a mere stranger to his humour; besides, I have some business invites me hence, with master Asinius Lupus, the tribune.

Tuc. Well, go thy ways, pursue thy projects, let me alone with this design; my Poetaster shall make thee a play, and thou shalt be a man of good parts in it. But stay, let me see; do not bring your

AEsop, your politician, unless you can ram up his mouth with
cloves; the slave smells ranker than some sixteen dunghills, and is
seventeen times more rotten. Marry, you may bring Frisker, my zany;
he's a good skipping swaggerer; and your fat fool there, my mango,
bring him too; but let him not beg rapiers nor scarfs, in his
over-familiar playing face, nor roar out his barren bold jests with
a tormenting laughter, between drunk and dry. Do you hear,
stiff-toe? give him warning, admonition, to forsake his saucy
glavering grace, and his goggle eye; it does not become him,
sirrah: tell him so. I have stood up and defended you, I, to
gentlemen, when you have been said to prey upon puisnes, and honest
citizens, for socks or buskins; or when they have call'd you
usurers or brokers, or said you were able to help to a piece of
flesh--I have sworn, I did not think so, nor that you were the
common retreats for punks decayed in their practice; I cannot
believe it of you.

Hist. Thank you, captain. Jupiter and the rest of the gods confine
your modern delights without disgust.

Tuc. Stay, thou shalt see the Moor ere thou goest.
                      [Enter DEMETRIUS at a distance.
What's he with the half arms there, that salutes us out of his
cloak, like a motion, ha?

Hist. O, sir, his doublet's a little decayed; he is otherwise a
very simple honest fellow, sir, one Demetrius, a dresser of plays
about the town here; we have hired him to abuse Horace, and bring
him in, in a play, with all his gallants, as Tibullus, Mecaenas,
Cornelius Gallus, and the rest.

Tuc. And why so, stinkard?

Hist. O, it will get us a huge deal of money, captain, and we have need on't; for this winter has made us all poorer than so many starved snakes: nobody comes at us, not a gentleman, nor a--

Tuc. But you know nothing by him, do you, to make a play of?

Hist. Faith, not much, captain; but our author will devise that that shall serve in some sort.

Tuc. Why, my Parnassus here shall help him, if thou wilt. Can thy author do it impudently enough?

Hist. O, I warrant you, captain, and spitefully enough too; he has one of tho most overflowing rank wits in Rome; he will slander any man that breathes, if he disgust him.

Tuc. I'll know the poor, egregious, nitty rascal; an he have these commendable qualities, I'll cherish him--stay, here comes the Tartar--I'll make a gathering for him, I, a purse, and put the poor slave in fresh rags; tell him so to comfort him.--
                    [Demetrius comes forward.

            Be-enter Minos, with 2 Pyrgus on his shoulders, and stalks
                    backward and forward, as the boy acts.

Well said, boy.

2 *Pyr.*
    Where art thou, boy? where is Calipolis?
    Fight earthquakes in the entrails of the earth,
    And eastern whirlwinds in the hellish shades;
    Some foul contagion of the infected heavens
    Blast all the trees, and in their cursed tops

The dismal night raven and tragic owl
Breed and become forerunners of my fall!

Tuc. Well, now fare thee well, my honest penny-biter: commend me to seven shares and a half, and remember to-morrow.--If you lack a service, you shall play in my name, rascals; but you shall buy your own cloth, and I'll have two shares for my countenance. Let thy author stay with me.
       [Exit Histrio.

Dem. Yes, sir.

Tuc. 'Twas well done, little Minos, thou didst stalk well: forgive me that I said thou stunk'st; Minos; 'twas the savour of a poet I met sweating in the street, hangs yet in my nostrils.

Cris. Who, Horace?

Tuc. Ay, he; dost thou know him?

Cris. O, he forsook me most barbarously, I protest.

Tuc. Hang him, fusty satyr, he smells all goat; he carries a ram under his arm-holes, the slave: I am the worse when I see him.-- Did not Minos impart?   [Aside to Crispinus.

Cris. Yes, here are twenty drachms he did convey.

Tuc. Well said, keep them, we'll share anon; come, little Minos.

Cris. Faith, captain, I'll be bold to shew you a mistress of mine, a jeweller's wife, a gallant, as we go along.

Tuc. There spoke my genius. Minos, some of thy eringos, little

Minos; send. Come hither, Parnassus, I must have thee familiar with my little locust here; 'tis a good vermin, they say.--

[Horace and Trebatius pass over the stage.]

See, here's Horace, and old Trebatius, the great lawyer, in his company; let's avoid him now, he is too well seconded.

[Exeunt.

ACT IV

SCENE I.-A Room in ALBIUS'S House.
enter CHLOE, CYTHERIS, and Attendants.

Chloe. But, sweet lady, say; am I well enough attired for the court, in sadness?

Cyth. Well enough! excellent well, sweet mistress Chloe; this strait-bodied city attire, I can tell you, will stir a courtier's blood, more than the finest loose sacks the ladies use to be put in; and then you are as well jewell'd as any of them; your ruff and linen about you is much more pure than theirs; and for your beauty, I can tell you, there's many of them would defy the painter, if they could change with you. Marry, the worst is, you must look to be envied, and endure a few court-frumps for it.

Chloe. O Jove, madam, I shall buy them too cheap!--Give me my muff, and my dog there.-And will the ladies be any thing familiar with me, think you?

Cyth. O Juno! why you shall see them flock about you with their puff-wings, and ask you where you bought your lawn, and what you paid for it? who starches you? and entreat you to help 'em to some pure laundresses out of the city.

Chloe. O Cupid!--Give me my fan, and my mask too.--And will the lords, and the poets there, use one well too, lady?

Cyth. Doubt not of that; you shall have kisses from them, go pit-pat, pit-pat, pit-pat, upon your lips, as thick as stones out of slings at the assault of a city. And then your ears will be so furr'd with the breath of their compliments, that you cannot catch cold of your head, if you would, in three winters after.

Chloe. Thank you, sweet lady. O heaven! and how must one behave herself amongst 'em? You know all.

Cyth. Faith, impudently enough, mistress Chloe, and well enough. Carry not too much under thought betwixt yourself and them; nor your city-mannerly word, forsooth, use it not too often in any case; but plain, Ay, madam, and no, madam: nor never say, your lordship, nor your honour; but, you, and you, my lord, and my lady: the other they count too simple and minsitive. And though they desire to kiss heaven with their titles, yet they will count them fools that give them too humbly.

Chloe. O intolerable, Jupiter! by my troth, lady, I would not for a world but you had lain in my house; and, i'faith, you shall not pay a farthing for your board, nor your chambers.

Cyth. O, sweet mistress Chloe! *Chloe.* I'faith you shall not, lady; nay, good lady, do not offer it.
[Enter GALLUS and TIBULLUS.
Gal. Come, where be these ladies? By your leave, bright stars, this gentleman and I are come to man you to court; where your late kind entertainment is now to be requited with a heavenly banquet.

Cyth. A heavenly banquet; Gallus!

Gal. No less, my dear Cytheris.

Tib. That were not strange, lady, if the epithet were only given for the company invited thither; your self, and this fair gentle-woman.

Chloe. Are we invited to court, sir?

Tib. You are, lady, by the great princess Julia; who longs to greet you with any favours that may worthily make you an often courtier.

Chloe. In sincerity, I thank her, sir. You have a coach, have you not?

Tib. The princess hath sent her own, lady.

Chloe. O Venus! that's well: I do long to ride in a coach most vehemently.

Cyth. But, sweet Gallus, pray you resolve me why you give that heavenly praise to this earthly banquet?

Gal. Because, Cytheris, it must be celebrated by the heavenly powers: all the gods and goddesses will be there; to two of which you two must be exalted.

Chloe. A pretty fiction, in truth.

Cyth. A fiction, indeed, Chloe, and fit for the fit of a poet.

Gal. Why, Cytheris, may not poets (from whose divine spirits all the honours of the gods have been deduced) entreat so much honour of the gods, to have their divine presence at a poetical banquet?

Cyth. Suppose that no fiction; yet, where are your habilities to make us two goddesses at your feast?

Gal. Who knows not, Cytheris, that the sacred breath of a true poet can blow any virtuous humanity up to deity?

Tib. To tell you the female truth, which is the simple truth, ladies; and to shew that poets, in spite of the world, are able to deify themselves; at this banquet, to which you are invited, we intend to assume the figures of the gods; and to give our several loves the forms of goddesses. Ovid will be Jupiter; the princess Julia, Juno; Gallus here, Apollo; you, Cytheris, Pallas; I will be Bacchus; and my love Plautia, Ceres: and to install you and your husband, fair Chloe, in honours equal with ours, you shall be a goddess, and your husband a god.

Chloe. A god!--O my gods!

Tib. A god, but a lame god, lady; for he shall be Vulcan, and you Venus: and this will make our banquet no less than heavenly.

Chloe. In sincerity, it will be sugared. Good Jove, what a pretty foolish thing it is to be a poet! but, hark you, sweet Cytheris, could they not possibly leave out my husband? methinks a body's husband does not so well at court; a body's friend, or so--but, husband! 'tis like your clog to your marmoset, for all the world, and the heavens.

Cyth. Tut, never fear, Chloe! your husband will be left without in the lobby, or the great chamber, when you shall be put in, i'the closet, by this lord, and by that lady.

Chloe. Nay, then I am certified; he shall go.
[Enter HORACE.

Gal. Horace! welcome.

Hor. Gentlemen, hear you the news?

Tib. What news, my Quintus!

Hor.
  Our melancholic friend, Propertius,
  Hath closed himself up in his Cynthia's tomb;
  And will by no entreaties be drawn thence.
    [Enter Albius, introducing CRISPINUS and DEMETRIUS,
      followed by Tucca.

Alb. Nay, good Master Crispinus, pray you bring near the gentleman.
[Going

Hor. Crispinus! Hide me, good Gallus; Tibullus, shelter me.

Cris. Make your approach, sweet captain.

Tib. What means this, Horace?

Hor. I am surprised again; farewell.

Gal. Stay, Horace.
[Exit hastily.

Tib 'Slight, I hold my life
  This same is he met him in Holy-street.

Hor. What, and be tired on by yond' vulture! No: Phoebus defend me!

Gal. Troth, 'tis like enough.--This act of Propertius relisheth very strange with me.

Tuc. By thy leave, my neat scoundrel: what, is this the mad boy you talk'd on?

Cris. Ay, this is master Albius, captain.

Tuc. Give me thy hand, Agamemnon; we hear abroad thou art the Hector of citizens: What sayest thou? are we welcome to thee, noble Neoptolemus?

Alb. Welcome, captain, by Jove and all the gods in the Capitol--

Tuc. No more, we conceive thee. Which of these is thy wedlock, Menelaus? thy Helen, thy Lucrece? that we may do her honour, mad boy.

Cris. She in the little fine dressing, sir, is my mistress.

Alb. For fault of a better, sir.

Tuc. A better! profane rascal: I cry thee mercy, my good scroyle, was't thou?

Alb. No harm, captain.

Tuc. She is a Venus, a Vesta, a Melpomene: come hither, Penelope; what's thy name, Iris?

Chloe. My name is Chloe, sir; I am a gentlewoman.

Tuc. Thou art in merit to be an empress, Chloe, for an eye and a lip; thou hast an emperor's nose: kiss me again: 'tis a virtuous punk; so! Before Jove, the gods were a sort of goslings, when they suffered so sweet a breath to perfume the bed of a stinkard: thou hadst ill fortune, Thisbe; the Fates were infatuate, they were, punk, they were.

Chloe. That's sure, sir: let me crave your name, I pray you, sir.

Tuc. I am known by the name of Captain Tucca, punk; the noble Roman, punk: a gentleman, and a commander, punk.
                             [Walks aside.
Chloe. In good time: a gentleman, and a commander! that's as good as a poet, methinks.

Cris. A pretty instrument! It's my cousin Cytheris' viol this, is it not?

Cyth. Nay, play, cousin; it wants but such a voice and hand to grace it, as yours is.

Cris. Alas, cousin, you are merrily inspired.

Cyth. Pray you play, if you love me.

Cris. Yes, cousin; you know I do not hate you.

Tib. A most subtile wench! how she hath baited him with a viol yonder, for a song!

Cris. Cousin, 'pray you call mistress Chloe! she shall hear an essay of my poetry.

Tuc. I'll call her.--Come hither, cockatrice: here's one will set thee up, my sweet punk, set thee up.

Chloe. Are you a poet so soon, sir?

      CRISPINUS plays and sings.

    Love is blind, and a wanton;
    In the whole world, there is scant one
      ---Such another:
      No, not his mother.
    He hath pluck'd her doves and sparrows,
    To feather his sharp arrows,
      And alone prevaileth,
      While sick Venus waileth.
    But if Cypris once recover
    The wag; it shall behove her
      To look better to him:
      Or she will undo him.

Alb. Wife, mum.

Alb. O, most odoriferous music!

Tuc. Aha, stinkard! Another Orpheus, you slave, another Orpheus! an Arion riding on the back of a dolphin, rascal!

Gal. Have you a copy of this ditty, sir?

Cris. Master Albius has.

Alb. Ay, but in truth they are my Wife's verses; I must not shew them.

Tuc. Shew them, bankrupt, shew them; they have salt in them, and will brook the air, stinkard.

Gal. How! To his bright mistress Canidia!

Cris. Ay, sir, that's but a borrowed name; as Ovid's Corinna, or Propertius his Cynthia, or your Nemesis, or Delia, Tibullus.

Gal. It's the name of Horace his witch, as I remember.

Tib. Why, the ditty's all borrowed; 'tis Horace's: hang him, plagiary!

Tut. How! he borrow of Horace? he shall pawn himself to ten brokers first. Do you hear, Poetasters? I know you to be men of worship--He shall write with Horace, for a talent! and let Mecaenas and his whole college of critics take his part: thou shalt do't, young Phoebus; thou shalt, Phaeton, thou shalt.

Dem. Alas, sir, Horace! he is a mere sponge; nothing but Humours and observation; he goes up and down sucking from every society, and when he comes home squeezes himself dry again. I know him, I.

Tuc. Thou say'st true, my poor poetical fury, he will pen all he knows. A sharp thorny-tooth, a satirical rascal, By him; he carries hay in his horn: he will sooner lose his best friend, than his least jest. What he once drops upon paper, against a man, lives eternally to upbraid him in the mouth of every slave, tankard-bearer, or waterman; not a bawd, or a boy that comes from the bake-house, but shall point at him: 'tis all dog, and scorpion; he carries poison in his teeth, and a sting in his tail. Fough! body of Jove! I'll have the slave whipt one of these days for his Satires and his Humours, by one cashier'd clerk or another.

Cris. We'll undertake him, captain.

Dem. Ay, and tickle him i'faith, for his arrogancy and his impudence, in commending his own things; and for his translating, I can trace him, i'faith. O, he is the most open fellow living; I had as lieve as a new suit I were at it.

Tuc. Say no more then, but do it; 'tis the only way to get thee a new suit; sting him, my little neufts; I'll give you instructions: I'll be your intelligencer; we'll all join, and hang upon him like so many horse-leeches, the players and all. We shall sup together, soon; and then we'll conspire, i'faith.

Gal. O that Horace had stayed still here!

Tib. So would not I; for both these would have turn'd Pythagoreans then.

Gal. What, mute?

Tib. Ay, as fishes, i'faith: come, ladies, shall we go?

Cyth. We wait you, sir. But mistress Chloe asks, if you have not a god to spare for this gentleman.

Gal. Who, captain Tucca?

Cyth. Ay, he.

Gal. Yes, if we can invite him along, he shall be Mars.

Chloe. Has Mars any thing to do with Venus?

Tib. O, most of all, lady.

Chloe. Nay, then I pray let him be invited: And what shall Crispinus be?

Tib. Mercury, mistress Chloe.

Chloe. Mercury! that's a poet, is it?

Gal. No, lady, but somewhat inclining that way; he is a herald at arms.

Chloe. A herald at arms! good; and Mercury! pretty: he has to do with Venus too?

Tib. A little with her face, lady; or so.

Chloe. 'Tis very well; pray let us go, I long to be at it.

Cyth. Gentlemen, shall we pray your companies along?

Cris. You shall not only pray, but prevail, lady.--Come, sweet captain.

Tuc. Yes, I follow: but thou must not talk of this now, my little bankrupt.

Alb. Captain, look here, mum.

Dem. I'll go write, sir.
[Exeunt.

SCENE II.-A Room in Lupus's House.
Enter Lupus, HISTRIO, and Lictors.

Tuc. Do, do: stay, there's a drachm to purchase ginger-bread for thy muse.

Lup. Come, let us talk here; here we may be private; shut the door, lictor. You are a player, you say.

Hist. Ay, an't please your worship.

Lup. Good; and how are you able to give this intelligence?

Hist. Marry, sir, they directed a letter to me and my fellow-- sharers.

Lup. Speak lower, you are not now in your theatre, stager:--my sword, knave. They directed a letter to you, and your fellow-sharers: forward.

Hist. Yes, sir, to hire some of our properties; as a sceptre and crown for Jove; and a caduceus for Mercury; and a petasus--
[Reenter Lictor.
Lup. Caduceus and petasus! let me see your letter. This is a conjuration: a conspiracy, this. Quickly, on with my buskins: I'll act a tragedy, i'faith. Will nothing but our gods serve these poets to profane? dispatch! Player, I thank thee. The emperor shall take knowledge of thy good service. [A knocking within.] Who's there now? Look, knave. [Exit Lictor.] A crown and a sceptre! this is good rebellion, now.

Lic. 'Tis your pothecary, sir, master Minos.

Lup. What tell'st thou me of pothecaries, knave! Tell him, I have affairs of state in hand; I can talk to no apothecaries now. Heart of me! Stay the pothecary there. [Walks in a musing posture.] You shall see, I have fish'd out a cunning piece of plot now: they have had some intelligence, that their project is discover'd, and now have they dealt with my apothecary, to poison me; 'tis so; knowing that I meant to take physic to-day: as sure as death, 'tis there. Jupiter, I thank thee, that thou hast. yet made me so much of a politician.

[Enter Minos.

You are welcome, sir; take the potion from him there; I have an antidote more than you wot of, sir; throw it on the ground there: so! Now fetch in the dog; and yet we cannot tarry to try experiments now: arrest him; you shall go with me, sir; I'll tickle you, pothecary; I'll give you a glister, i'faith. Have I the letter? ay, 'tis here.--Come, your fasces, lictors: the half pikes and the Halberds, take them down from the Lares there. Player, assist me.

[As they are going out, enter MECAENAS and HORACE.

Mec. Whither now, Asinius Lupus, with this armory?

Lup. I cannot talk now; I charge you assist me: treason! treason!

Hor. How! treason?

Lup. Ay: if you love the emperor, and the state, follow me.

[Exeunt.

SCENE III.-An Apartment in the Palace.

Enter OVID, JULIA, GALLUS, CYTHERIS, TIBULLUS, PLAUTIA, ALBIUS, CHLOE, TUCCA, CRISPINUS, HERMOGENES, PYRGUS, *characteristically habited, as gods and goddesses.*

Ovid. Gods and goddesses, take your several seats. Now, Mercury, move your caduceus, and, in Jupiter's name, command silence.

Cris. In the name of Jupiter, silence.

Her. The crier of the court hath too clarified a voice.

Gal. Peace, Momus.

Ovid. Oh, he is the god of reprehension; let him alone: 'tis his office. Mercury, go forward, and proclaim, after Phoebus, our high pleasure, to all the deities that shall partake this high banquet.

Cris. Yes, sir.

Gal. The great god, Jupiter,--[Here, and at every break in the line, Crispinus repeats aloud the words of Gallus.]--Of his licentious goodness,--Willing to make this feast no fast--From any manner of pleasure;--Nor to bind any god or goddess--To be any thing the more god or goddess, for their names:--He gives them all free license--To speak no wiser than persons of baser titles;-- And to be nothing better, than common men, or women.--And therefore no god--Shall need to keep himself more strictly to his goddess--Than any man does to his wife:--Nor any goddess--Shall need to keep herself more strictly to her god--Than any woman does to her husband.--But, since it is no part of wisdom,--In these days, to come into bonds;--It shall be lawful for every lover--To break loving oaths,--To change their lovers, and make love to others,--As the heat of every one's blood,--And the spirit of our nectar, shall inspire.--And Jupiter save Jupiter!

Tib. So; now we may play the fools by authority.

Her. To play the fool by authority is wisdom.

Jul. Away with your mattery sentences, Momus; they are too grave and wise for this meeting.

Ovid. Mercury, give our jester a stool, let him sit by; and reach him one of our cates.

Tuc. Dost hear, mad Jupiter? we'll have it enacted, he that speaks the first wise word, shall be made cuckold. What say'st thou? Is it not a good motion?

Ovid. Deities, are you all agreed?

All, Agreed, great Jupiter.

Alb. I have read in a book, that to play the fool wisely, is high wisdom.

Gal. How now, Vulcan! will you be the first wizard?

Ovid. Take his wife, Mars, and make him cuckold quickly.

Tuc. Come, cockatrice.

Chloe. No, let me alone with him, Jupiter: I'll make you take heed, sir, while you live again; if there be twelve in a company, that you be not the wisest of 'em.

Alb. No more; I will not indeed, wife, hereafter; I'll be here: mum.

Ovid. Fill us a bowl of nectar, Ganymede: we will drink to our daughter Venus.

Gal. Look to your wife, Vulcan: Jupiter begins to court her.

Tib. Nay, let Mars look to it: Vulcan must do as Venus does, bear.

Tuc. Sirrah, boy; catamite: Look you play Ganymede well now, you slave. Do not spill your nectar; carry your cup even: so! You should have rubbed your face with whites of eggs, you rascal; till your brows had shone like our sooty brother's here, as sleek as a horn-book: or have steept your lips in wine, till you made them so plump, that Juno might have been jealous of them. Punk, kiss me, punk.

Ovid. Here, daughter Venus, I drink to thee.

Chloe. Thank you, good father Jupiter.

Tuc. Why, mother Juno! gods and fiends! what, wilt thou suffer this ocular temptation?

Tib. Mars is enraged, he looks big, and begins to stut for anger.

Her. Well played, captain Mars.

Tuc. Well said, minstrel Momus: I must put you in, must I? when will you be in good fooling of yourself, fidler, never?

Her. O, 'tis our fashion to be silent, when there is a better fool in place ever.

Tuc. Thank you, rascal.

Ovid. Fill to our daughter Venus, Ganymede, who fills her father with affection.

Jul. Wilt thou be ranging, Jupiter, before my face?

Ovid. Why not, Juno? why should Jupiter stand in awe of thy face, Juno?

Jul. Because it is thy wife's face, Jupiter.

Ovid. What, shall a husband be afraid of his wife's face? will she paint it so horribly? we are a king, cotquean; and we will reign in our pleasures; and we will cudgel thee to death, if thou find fault with us.

Jul. I will find fault with thee, king cuckold-maker: What, shall the king of gods turn the king of good-fellows, and have no fellow in wickedness? This makes our poets, that know our profaneness, live as profane as we: By my godhead, Jupiter, 1 will join with all the other gods here, bind thee hand and foot, throw thee down into the earth and make a poor poet of thee, if thou abuse me thus.

Gal. A good smart-tongued goddess, a right Juno!

Ovid. Juno, we will cudgel thee, Juno: we told thee so yesterday, when thou wert jealous of us for Thetis.

Pyr. Nay, to-day she had me in inquisition too.

Tuc. Well said, my fine Phrygian fry; inform, inform. Give me some wine, king of heralds, I may drink to my cockatrice.

Ovid. No more, Ganymede; we will cudgel thee, Juno; by Styx we will.

Jul. Ay, 'tis well; gods may grow impudent in iniquity, and they must not be told of it

Ovid. Yea, we will knock our chin against our breast, and shake thee out of Olympus into an oyster-boat, for thy scolding.

Jul. Your nose is not long enough to do it, Jupiter, if all thy strumpets thou hast among the stars took thy part. And there is never a star in thy forehead but shall be a horn, if thou persist to abuse me.

Cris. A good jest, i'faith.

Ovid. We tell thee thou angerest us, cotquean; and we will thunder thee in pieces for thy cotqueanity.

Cris. Another good jest.

Alb. O, my hammers and my Cyclops! This boy fills not wine enough to make us kind enough to one another.

Tuc. Nor thou hast not collied thy face enough, stinkard.

Alb. I'll ply the table with nectar, and make them friends.

Her. Heaven is like to have but a lame skinker, then.

Alb. Wine and good livers make true lovers: I'll sentence them together. Here, father, here, mother, for shame, drink yourselves drunk, and forget this dissension; you two should cling together before our faces, and give us example of unity.

Gal O, excellently spoken, Vulcan, on the sudden!

Tib. Jupiter may do well to prefer his tongue to some office for his eloquence. Tuc. His tongue shall be gentleman-usher to his wit, and still go before it.

Alb. An excellent fit office!

Cris. Ay, and an excellent good jest besides.

Her. What, have you hired Mercury to cry your jests you make?

Ovid. Momus, you are envious.

Tuc. Why, ay, you whoreson blockhead, 'tis your only block of wit in fashion now-a-days, to applaud other folks' jests.

Her. True; with those that are not artificers themselves. Vulcan, you nod, and the mirth of the jest droops.

Pyr. He has filled nectar so long, till his brain swims in it.

Gal. What, do we nod, fellow-gods! Sound music, and let us startle our spirits with a song.

Tuc. Do, Apollo, thou art a good musician.

Gal. What says Jupiter?

Ovid. Ha! ha!

Gal. A song.

Ovid. Why, do, do, sing.

Pla. Bacchus, what say you?

Tib. Ceres?

Pla. But, to this song?

Tib. Sing, for my part.

Jul. Your belly weighs down your head, Bacchus; here's a song toward.

Tib. Begin, Vulcan.

Alb. What else, what else?

Tuc. Say, Jupiter

Ovid. Mercury---

Cris. Ay, say, say.

                              [Music

Alb.   Wake! our mirth begins to die;

        Quicken it with tunes and wine.
       Raise your notes; you're out; fie, fie!
         This drowsiness is an ill sign.
       We banish him the quire of gods,
           That droops agen:
           Then all are men,
      For here's not one but nods.

Ovid. I like not this sudden and general heaviness amongst our godheads; 'tis somewhat ominous. Apollo, command us louder music, and let Mercury and Momus contend to please and revive our senses.
                              [Music

Herm.   Then, in a free and lofty strain.
              Our broken tunes we thus repair;
Cris.   And we answer them again,
              Running division on the panting air;
Ambo.   To celebrate this, feast of sense,
              As free from scandal as offence.
Herm.   Here is beauty for the eye,
Cris.   For the ear sweet melody.
Herm.   Ambrosiac odours, for the smell,
Cris.   Delicious nectar, for the taste;
Ambo.   For the touch, a lady's waist;
            Which doth all the rest excel.

Ovid. Ay, this has waked us. Mercury, our herald; go from ourself, the great god Jupiter, to the great emperor Augustus Caesar, and command him from us, of whose bounty he hath received the sirname of Augustus, that, for a thank-offering to our beneficence, he presently sacrifice, as a dish to this banquet, his beautiful and wanton daughter Julia: she's a curst quean, tell him, and plays the scold behind his back;

therefore let her be sacrificed. Command him this, Mercury, in our high name of Jupiter Altitonans.

Jul. Stay, feather-footed Mercury, and tell Augustus, from us, the great Juno Saturnia; if he think it hard to do as Jupiter hath commanded him, and sacrifice his daughter, that he had better do so ten times, than suffer her to love the well-nosed poet, Ovid; whom he shall do well to whip or cause to be whipped, about the capitol, for soothing her in her follies.

[Enter AUGUSTUS CAESAR, MECAENAS, HORACE, LUPUS, HISTRIO, MINUS, and Lictors.

Caes.
What sight is this? Mecaenas! Horace! say?
Have we our senses? do we hear and see?
Or are these but imaginary objects
Drawn by our phantasy! Why speak you not?
Let us do sacrifice. Are they the gods?
    [Ovid and the rest kneel.
Reverence, amaze, and fury fight in me.
What, do they kneel! Nay, then I see 'tis true
I thought impossible: O, impious sight!
Let me divert mine eyes; the very thought
Everts my soul with passion: Look not, man,
There is a panther, whose unnatural eyes
Will strike thee dead: turn, then, and die on her
With her own death.
    [Offers to kill his daughter.
Mec. Hor. What means imperial Caesar?

Caes. What would you have me let the strnmpet live That, for this pageant, earns so many deaths?

Tuc. Boy, slink, boy.

THE POETASTER OR HIS ARRAIGNMENT 125

[Exeunt Tucca and Pyrgus.
Pyr. Pray Jupiter we be not followed by the scent, master.

Caes. Say, sir, what are you?

Alb. I play Vulcan, sir.

Caes. But what are you, sir?

Alb. Your citizen and jeweller, sir.

Caes. And what are you, dame?

Chloe. I play Venus, forsooth.

Caes. I ask not what you play, but what you are.

Chloe. Your citizen and jeweller's wife, sir.

Caes. And you, good sir?
          [Exit.
Caes.
 O, that profaned name!---
 And are these seemly company for thee, [To Julia.
 Degenerate monster? All the rest I know,
 And hate all knowledge for their hateful sakes.
 Are you, that first the deities inspired
 With skill of their high natures and their powers,
 The first abusers of their useful light;
 Profaning thus their dignities in their forms,
 And making them, like you, but counterfeits?
 O, who shall follow Virtue and embrace her,
 When her false bosom is found nought but air?

And yet of those embraces centaurs spring,
That war with human peace, and poison men.---
Who shall, with greater comforts comprehend
Her unseen being and her excellence;
When you, that teach, and should eternise her,
Live as she were no law unto your lives,
Nor lived herself, but with your idle breaths?
If you think gods but feign'd, and virtue painted,
Know we sustain an actual residence,
And with the title of an emperor,
Retain his spirit and imperial power;
By which, in imposition too remiss,
Licentious Naso, for thy violent wrong,
In soothing the declined affections
Of our base daughter, we exile thy feet
From all approach to our imperial court,
On pain of death; and thy misgotten love
Commit to patronage of iron doors;
Since her soft-hearted sire cannot contain her.

Cris. Your gentleman parcel-poet, sir.

Mec. O, good my lord, forgive! be like the gods.

Hor. Let royal bounty, Caesar, mediate.

Caes.
There is no bounty to be shew'd to such
As have no real goodness: bounty is
A spice of virtue; and what virtuous act
Can take effect on them, that have no power
Of equal habitude to apprehend it,
But live in worship of that idol, vice,

As if there were no virtue, but in shade
Of strong imagination, merely enforced ?
This shews their knowledge is mere ignorance,
Their far-fetch'd dignity of soul a fancy,
And all their square pretext of gravity
A mere vain-glory; hence, away with them!
I will prefer for knowledge, none but such
As rule their lives by it, and can becalm
All sea of Humour with the marble trident
Of their strong spirits: others fight below
With gnats and shadows; others nothing know.
                    [Exeunt.

SCENE IV.-A Street before the Palace.
Enter TUCCA, CRISPINUS, and PYRGUS.

Tuc. What's become of my little punk, Venus, and the poultfoot stinkard, her husband, ha?

Cris. O; they are rid home in the coach, as fast as the wheels can run.

Tuc. God Jupiter is banished, I hear, and his cockatrice Juno lock'd up. 'Heart, an all the poetry in Parnassus get me to be a player again, I'll sell 'em my share for a sesterce. But this is Humours, Horace, that goat-footed envious slave; he's turn'd fawn now; an informer, the rogue! 'tis he has betray'd us all. Did you not see him with the emperor crouching?

Cris. Yes.

Tuc. Well, follow me. Thou shalt libel, and I'll cudgel the rascal. Boy, provide me a truncheon. Revenge shall gratulate him, tam Marti, quam Mercurio.

Pyr. Ay, but master, take heed how you give this out; Horace is a man of the sword.

Cris. 'Tis true, in troth; they say he's valiant.

[Horace passes over the stage.

Tuc. Valiant? so is mine a--. Gods and fiends! I'll blow him into air when I meet him next: he dares not fight with a puck-fist.

Pyr. Master, he comes!

Tuc. Where? Jupiter save thee, my good poet, my noble prophet, my little fat Horace.--I scorn to beat the rogue in the court; and I saluted him thus fair, because he should suspect nothing, the rascal. Come, we'll go see how far forward our journeyman is toward the untrussing of him.

[Exeunt.

SCENE V.
Enter HORACE, MECAENAS, LUPUS, HISTRIO, and Lictors.

Cris. Do you hear, captain? I'll write nothing in it but innocence, because I may swear I am innocent.

Hor. Nay, why pursue you not the emperor for your reward now, Lupus?

Mec.
  Stay, Asinius;
  You and your stager, and your band of lictors:
  I hope your service merits more respect,
  Than thus, without a thanks, to be sent hence.

His. Well, well, jest on, jest on.

Hor. Thou base, unworthy groom!

Lup. Ay, ay, 'tis good.

Hor.
  Was this the treason, this the dangerous plot,
  Thy clamorous tongue so bellow'd through the court?
  Hadst thou no other project to encrease
  Thy grace with Caesar, but this wolfish train,
  To prey upon the life of innocent mirth
  And harmless pleasures, bred of noble wit? Away!
  I loath thy presence; such as thou,
  They are the moths and scarabs of a state,

The bane of empires, and the dregs of courts;
Who, to endear themselves to an employment,
Care not whose fame they blast, whose life they endanger;
And, under a disguised and cobweb mask
Of love unto their sovereign, vomit forth
Their own prodigious malice; and pretending
To be the props and columns of their safety,
The guards unto his person and his peace.
Disturb it most, with their false, lapwing-cries.

Lup. Good! Caesar shall know of this, believe it!

Mec.
  Caesar doth know it, wolf, and to his knowledge,
He will, I hope, reward your base endeavours.
Princes that will but hear, or give access
To such officious spies, can ne'er be safe:
They take in poison with an open ear,
And, free from danger, become slaves to fear.
                            [Exeunt.

SCENE VI.-An open Space before the Palace.
Enter OVID.

Banish'd the court! Let me be banish'd life,
Since the chief end of life is there concluded:
Within the court is all the kingdom bounded,
And as her sacred sphere doth comprehend
Ten thousand times so much, as so much place
In any part of all the empire else;
So every body, moving in her sphere,
Contains ten thousand times as much in him,
As any other her choice orb excludes.
As in a circle, a magician then
Is safe against the spirit he excites;
But, out of it, is subject to his rage,
And loseth all the virtue of his art:
So I, exiled the circle of the court,
Lose all the good gifts that in it I 'joy'd.
No virtue current is, but with her stamp,
And no vice vicious, blanch'd with her white hand.
The court's the abstract of all Rome's desert,
And my dear Julia the abstract of the court.
Methinks, now I come near her, I respire
Some air of that late comfort I received;
And while the evening, with her modest veil,
Gives leave to such poor shadows as myself
To steal abroad, I, like a heartless ghost,
Without the living body of my love,
Will here walk and attend her: for I know
Not far from hence she is imprisoned,
And hopes, of her strict guardian, to bribe

So much admittance, as to speak to me,
And cheer my fainting spirits with her breath.

Julia. [appears above at her chamber window.] Ovid? my love?

Ovid. Here, heavenly Julia.

Jul.
Here! and not here! O, how that word doth play
With both our fortunes, differing, like ourselves,
Both one; and yet divided, as opposed!
I high, thou low: O, this our plight of place
Doubly presents the two lets of our love,
Local and ceremonial height, and lowness:
Both ways, I am too high, and thou too low,
Our minds are even yet; O, why should our bodies,
That are their slaves, be so without their rule?
I'll cast myself down to thee; if I die,
I'll ever live with thee: no height of birth,
Of place, of duty, or of cruel power,
Shall keep me from thee; should my father lock
This body up within a tomb of brass,
Yet I'll be with thee. If the forms I hold
Now in my soul, be made one substance with it;
That soul immortal, and the same 'tis now;
Death cannot raze the affects she now retaineth:
And then, may she be any where she will.
The souls of parents rule not children's souls,
When death sets both in their dissolv'd estates;
Then is no child nor father; then eternity
Frees all from any temporal respect.
I come, my Ovid; take me in thine arms,
And let me breathe my soul into thy breast.

Ovid.
>O stay, my love; the hopes thou dost conceive
>Of thy quick death, and of thy future life,
>Are not authentical. Thou choosest death,
>So thou might'st 'joy thy love in the other life:
>But know, my princely love, when thou art dead,
>Thou only must survive in perfect soul;
>And in the soul are no affections.
>We pour out our affections with our blood,
>And, with our blood's affections, fade our loves.
>No life hath love in such sweet state as this;
>No essence is so dear to moody sense
>As flesh and blood, whose quintessence is sense.
>Beauty, composed of blood and flesh, moves more,
>And is more plausible to blood and flesh,
>Than spiritual beauty can be to the spirit.
>Such apprehension as we have in dreams,
>When, sleep, the bond of senses, locks them up,
>Such shall we have, when death destroys them quite.
>If love be then thy object, change not life;
>Live high and happy still: I still below,
>Close with my fortunes, in thy height shall joy.

Jul.
>Ay me, that virtue, whose brave eagle's wings,
>With every stroke blow stairs in burning heaven,
>Should, like a swallow, preying towards storms,
>Fly close to earth, and with an eager plume,
>Pursue those objects which none else can see,
>But seem to all the world the empty air!
>Thus thou, poor Ovid, and all virtuous men,
>Must prey, like swallows, on invisible food,

  Pursuing flies, or nothing: and thus love.
And every worldly fancy, is transposed
By worldly tyranny to what plight it list.
O father, since thou gav'st me not my mind,
Strive not to rule it; take but what thou gav'st
To thy disposure: thy affections
Rule not in me; I must bear all my griefs,
Let me use all my pleasures; virtuous love
Was never scandal to a goddess' state.--
But he's inflexible! and, my dear love,
Thy life may chance be shorten'd by the length
Of my unwilling speeches to depart.
Farewell, sweet life; though thou be yet exiled
The officious court, enjoy me amply still:
My soul, in this my breath, enters thine ears,
And on this turret's floor Will I lie dead,
Till we may meet again: In this proud height,
I kneel beneath thee in my prostrate love,
And kiss the happy sands that kiss thy feet.
Great Jove submits a sceptre to a cell,
And lovers, ere they part, will meet in hell.

Ovid.
  Farewell all company, and, if l could,
All light with thee! hell's shade should hide my brows,
Till thy dear beauty's beams redeem'd my vows.
          [Going

Jul.
  Ovid, my love; alas! may we not stay .
A little longer, think'st thou, undiscern'd?

Ovid.
  For thine own good, fair goddess, do not stay.

THE POETASTER OR HIS ARRAIGNMENT

   Who would engage a firmament of fires
   Shining in thee, for me, a falling star?
   Be gone, sweet life-blood; if I should discern
   Thyself but touch'd for my sake, I should die.

Jul.
   I will begone, then; and not heaven itself
   Shall draw me back.   [Going.

Ovid.
   Yet, Julia, if thou Wilt, A little longer stay.

Jul.
   I am content.

Ovid.
   O, mighty Ovid! what the sway of heaven
   Could not retire, my breath hath turned back.

Jul.
   Who shall go first, my love? my passionate eyes
   Will not endure to see thee turn from me.

Ovid.
   If thou go first, my soul
   Will follow thee.

Jul.
   Then we must stay.

Ovid.
   Ay me, there is no stay
   In amorous pleasures; if both stay, both die.

I hear thy father; hence, my deity.
                    [Julia retires from the window.
Fear forgeth sounds in my deluded ears;
I did not hear him; I am mad with love.
There is no spirit under heaven, that works
With such illusion; yet such witchcraft kill me,
Ere a sound mind, without it, save my life!
Here, on my knees, I worship the blest place
That held my goddess; and the loving air,
That closed her body in his silken arms.
Vain Ovid! kneel not to the place, nor air;
She's in thy heart; rise then, and worship there.
The truest wisdom silly men can have,
Is dotage on the follies of their flesh.   [Exit.

ACT V SCENE I.-An Apartment in the Palace.

Enter CAESAR, MECAENAS, GALLUS, TIBULLUS, HORACE, and Equites Romani.

Caes.
    We, that have conquer'd still, to save the conquer'd,
    And loved to make inflictions fear'd, not felt;
    Grieved to reprove, and joyful to reward;
    More proud of reconcilement than revenge;
    Resume into the late state of our love,
    Worthy Cornelius Gallus, and Tibullus:
    You both are gentlemen: and, you, Cornelius,
    A soldier of renown, and the first provost
    That ever let our Roman eagles fly
    On swarthy AEgypt, quarried with her spoils.
    Yet (not to bear cold forms, nor men's out-terms,
    Without the inward fires, and lives of men)
    You both have virtues shining through your shapes;
    To shew, your titles are not writ on posts,
    Or hollow statues which the best men are,
    Without Promethean stuffings reach'd from heaven!
    Sweet poesy's sacred garlands crown your gentry:
    Which is, of all the faculties on earth,
    The most abstract and perfect; if she be
    True-born, and nursed with all the sciences.
    She can so mould Rome, and her monuments,

Within the liquid marble of her lines,
That they shall stand fresh and miraculous,
Even when they mix with innovating dust;
In her sweet streams shall our brave Roman spirits
Chase, and swim after death, with their choice deeds
Shining on their white shoulders; and therein
Shall Tyber, and our famous rivers fall
With such attraction, that the ambitious line
Of the round world shall to her centre shrink,
To hear their music: and, for these high parts,
Caesar shall reverence the Pierian arts.

Mec.
Your majesty's high grace to poesy,
Shall stand 'gainst all the dull detractions
Of leaden souls; who, for the vain assumings
Of some, quite worthless of her sovereign wreaths,
Contain her worthiest prophets in contempt.
Gal. Happy is Rome of all earth's other states,
To have so true and great a president,
For her inferior spirits to imitate,
As Caesar is; who addeth to the sun
Influence and lustre; in increasing thus
His inspirations, kindling fire in us.

Hor.
Phoebus himself shall kneel at Caesar's shrine,
And deck it with bay garlands dew'd with wine,
To quit the worship Caesar does to him:
Where other princes, hoisted to their thrones
By Fortune's passionate and disorder'd power,
Sit in their height, like clouds before the sun,
Hindering his comforts; and, by their excess

Of cold in virtue, and cross heat in vice,
　　Thunder and tempest on those learned heads,
　　Whom Caesar with such honour doth advance.

Tib.
　　All human business fortune doth command
　　Without all order; and with her blind hand,
　　She, blind, bestows blind gifts, that still have nurst,
　　They see not who, nor how, but still, the worst.

Caes.
　　Caesar, for his rule, and for so much stuff
　　As Fortune puts in his hand, shall dispose it,
　　As if his hand had eyes and soul in it,
　　With worth and judgment. Hands, that part with gifts
　　Or will restrain their use, without desert,
　　Or with a misery numb'd to virtue's right,
　　Work, as they had no soul to govern them,
　　And quite reject her; severing their estates
　　From human order. Whosoever can,
　　And will not cherish virtue, is no man.
　　　　　　[Enter some of the Equestrian Order.
Eques. Virgil is now at hand, imperial Caesar.

Caes.
　　Rome's honour is at hand then. Fetch a chair,
　　And set it on our right hand, where 'tis fit
　　Rome's honour and our own should ever sit.
　　Now he is come out of Campania,
　　I doubt not he hath finish'd all his Æneids.
　　Which, like another soul, I long to enjoy.
　　What think you three of Virgil, gentlemen,
　　That are of his profession, though rank'd higher;

Or, Horace, what say'st thou, that art the poorest,
And likeliest to envy, or to detract

Hor.
    Caesar speaks after common men in this,
    To make a difference of me for my poorness;
    As if the filth of poverty sunk as deep
    Into a knowing spirit, as the bane
    Of riches doth into an ignorant soul.
    No, Caesar, they be pathless, moorish minds
    That being once made rotten with the dung
    Of damned riches, ever after sink
    Beneath the steps of any villainy.
    But knowledge is the nectar that keeps sweet
    A perfect soul, even in this grave of sin;
    And for my soul, it is as free as Caesar's,
    For what 1 know is due I'll give to all.
    He that detracts or envies virtuous merit,
    Is still the covetous and the ignorant spirit.

Caes.
    Thanks, Horace, for thy free and wholesome sharpness,
    Which pleaseth Caesar more than servile fawns.
    A flatter'd prince soon turns the prince of fools.
    And for thy sake, we'll put no difference more
    Between the great and good for being poor.
    Say then, loved Horace, thy true thought of Virgil.

Hor.
    I judge him of a rectified spirit,
    By many revolutions of discourse,
    (In his bright reason's influence,) refined
    From all the tartarous moods of common men;

Bearing the nature and similitude
Of a right heavenly body; most severe
In fashion and collection of himself;
And, then, as clear and confident as Jove.

Gal.
And yet so chaste and tender is his ear,
In suffering any syllable to pass,
That he thinks may become the honour'd name
Of issue to his so examined self,
That all the lasting fruits of his full merit,
In his own poems, he doth still distaste;
And if his mind's piece, which he strove to paint,
Could not with fleshly pencils have her right.

Tib.
But to approve his works of sovereign worth,
This observation, methinks, more than serves,
And is not vulgar. That which he hath writ
Is with such judgment labour'd, and distill'd
Through all the needful uses of our lives,
That could a man remember but his lines,
He should not touch at any serious point,
But he might breathe his spirit out of him.

Caes.
You mean, he might repeat part of his works,
As fit for any conference he can use?

Tib. True, royal Caesar.

Caes.
Worthily observed;

And a most worthy virtue in his works.
What thinks material Horace of his learning?

Hor.
His learning savours not the school-like gloss,
That most consists in echoing words and terms,
And soonest wins a man an empty name;
Nor any long or far-fetch'd circumstance
Wrapp'd in the curious generalties of arts;
But a direct and analytic sum
Of all the worth and first effects of arts.
And for his poesy, 'tis so ramm'd with life,
That it shall gather strength of life, with being,
And live hereafter more admired than now.

Caes.
This one consent in all your dooms of him,
And mutual loves of all your several merits,
Argues a truth of merit in you all.---
      [Enter VIRGIL.
See, here comes Virgil; we will rise and greet him.
Welcome to Caesar, Virgil! Caesar and Virgil
Shall differ but in sound; to Caesar, Virgil,
Of his expressed greatness, shall be made
A second sirname, and to Virgil, Caesar.
Where are thy famous AEneids? do us grace
To let us see, and surfeit on their sight.

Virg.
Worthless they are of Caesar's gracious eyes,
If they were perfect; much more with their wants,
Which are yet more than my time could supply.
And, could great Caesar's expectation

Be satisfied with any other service,
I would not shew them.

Caes.
Virgil is too modest;
Or seeks, in vain, to make our longings more:
Shew them, sweet Virgil.

Virg.
Then, in such due fear
As fits presenters of great works to Caesar,
I humbly shew them.

Caes.
Let us now behold
A human soul made visible in life;
And more refulgent in a senseless paper
Than in the sensual complement of kings.
Read, read thyself, dear Virgil; let not me
Profane one accent with an untuned tongue:
Best matter, badly shewn, shews worse than bad.
See then this chair, of purpose set for thee
To read thy poem in; refuse it not.
Virtue, without presumption, place may take
Above best kings, whom only she should make.

Virg.
It will be thought a thing ridiculous
To present eyes, and to all future times
A gross untruth, that any poet, void
Of birth, or wealth, or temporal dignity,
Should, with decorum, trauscend Caesar's chair.
Poor virtue raised, high birth and wealth set under,

Crosseth heaven's courses, and makes worldlings wonder.

Caes.
　The course of heaven, and fate itself, in this,
　Will Ceasar cross; much more all worldly custom.

Hor.
　Custom, in course of honour, ever errs;
　And they are best whom fortune least prefers.

Caes.
　Horace hath but more strictly spoke our thoughts.
　The vast rude swing of general confluence
　Is, in particular ends, exempt from sense:
　And therefore reason (which in right should be
　The special rector of all harmony)
　Shall shew we are a man distinct by it,
　From those, whom custom rapteth in her press.
　Ascend then, Virgil; and where first by chance
　We here have turn'd thy book, do thou first read.

Virg.
　Great Caesar hath his will; I will ascend.
　'Twere simple injury to his free hand,
　That sweeps the cobwebs from unused virtue,
　And makes her shine proportion'd to her worth,
　To be more nice to entertain his grace,
　Than he is choice, and liberal to afford it.

Caes.
　Gentlemen of our chamber, guard the doors,
　And let none enter;
　　　　　　　　　　　[Exeunt Equites.]

peace. Begin, good Virgil.

Virg.
   Meanwhile the skies 'gan thunder, and in tail
Of that, fell pouring storms of sleet and hail:
The Tyrian lords and Trojan youth, each where
With Venus' Dardane nephew, now, in fear,
Seek out for several shelter through the plain,
Whilst floods come rolling from the hills amain.
Dido a cave, the Trojan prince the same
Lighted upon. There earth and heaven's great dame,
That hath the charge of marriage, first gave sign
Unto his contract; fire and air did shine,
As guilty of the match; and from the hill
The nymphs with shriekings do the region fill.
Here first began their bane; this day was ground
Of all their ills; for now, nor rumour's sound,
Nor nice respect of state, moves Dido ought;
Her love no longer now by stealth is sought:
She calls this wedlock, and with that fair name
Covers her fault. Forthwith the bruit and fame,
Through all the greatest Lybian towns is gone;
Fame, a fleet evil, than which is swifter none,
That moving grows, and flying gathers strength,
Little at first, and fearful; but at length
She dares attempt the skies, and stalking proud
With feet on ground, her head doth pierce a cloud!
This child, our parent earth, stirr'd up with spite
Of all the gods, brought forth; and, as some write,
She was last sister of that giant race
That thought to scale Jove's court; right swift of pace,
And swifter far of wing; a monster vast,
And dreadful. Look, how many plumes are placed

On her huge corps, so many waking eyes
Stick underneath; and, which may stranger rise
In the report, as many tongues she bears,
As many mouths, as many listening ears.
Nightly, in midst of all the heaven, she flies,
And through the earth's dark shadow shrieking cries,
Nor do her eyes once bend to taste sweet sleep;
By day on tops of houses she doth keep,
Or on high towers; and doth thence affright
Cities and towns of most conspicuous site:
As covetous she is of tales and lies,
As prodigal of truth: this monster--

Lup. [within.] Come, follow me, assist me, second me! Where'! the emperor?

1 Eques. [within.] Sir, you must pardon us.

2 Eques. [within.] Caesar is private now; you may not enter.

Tuc. [within.] Not enter! Charge them upon their allegiance, cropshin.

1 Eques. [within.] We have a charge to the contrary, sir.

Lup. [within.] I pronounce you all traitors, horrible traitors: What! do you know my affairs? I have matter of danger and state to impart to Caesar.

Caes. What noise is there? who's that names Caesar?

Lup. [within.] A friend to Caesar. One that, for Caesar's good, would speak with Caesar.

Caes. Who is it? look, Cornelius.

1 Eques. [within.] Asinius Lupus.

Caes.
  O, bid the turbulent informer hence;
  We have no vacant ear now, to receive
  The unseason'd fruits of his officious tongue.

Mec. You must avoid him there.

Lup. [within.] I conjure thee, as thou art. Caesar, or respectest thine own safety, or the safety of the state, Caesar, hear me, speak with me, Caesar; 'tis no common business I come about, but such, as being neglected, may concern the life of Caesar.

Caes. The life of Caesar! Let him enter. Virgil, keep thy seat.
             Enter Lupus, Tucca, and Lictors.
Eques. [within.] Bear back, there: whither will you? keep back!

Tuc. By thy leave, goodman usher: mend thy peruke; so.

Lup. Lay hold on Horace there; and on Mecaenas, lictors. Romans, offer no rescue, upon your allegiance: read, royal Caesar. [Gives a paper.] I'll tickle you, Satyr.

Tuc. He will, Humours, he will; he will squeeze you, poet puck-fist.

Lup. I'll lop you off for an unprofitable branch, you satirical varlet.

Tuc. Ay, and Epaminondas your patron here, with his flagon chain;

come, resign: [takes off Mecaenas' chain,] though 'twere your great grandfather's, the law has made it mine now, sir. Look to him, my party-coloured rascals; look to him.

Caes. What is this, Asinius Lupus? I understand it not.

Lup. Not understand it! A libel, Caesar; a dangerous, seditious libel; a libel in picture.

Caes. A libel!

Lup. Ay, I found it in this Horace his study, in Mecaenas his house, here; I challenge the penalty of the laws against them.

Tuc. Ay, and remember to beg their land betimes; before some of these hungry court-hounds scent it out.

Caes. Shew it to Horace: ask him if he know it.

Lup. Know it! his hand is at it, Caesar.

Caes. Then 'tis no libel.

Hor. It is the imperfect body of an emblem, Caesar, I began for Mecaenas.

Lup. An emblem! right: that's Greek for a libel. Do but mark how confident he is.

Hor.
  A just man cannot fear, thou foolish tribune;
  Not, though the malice of traducing tongues,
  The open vastness of a tyrant's ear,

The senseless rigour of the wrested laws,
Or the red eyes of strain'd authority,
Should, in a point, meet all to take his life:
His innocence is armour 'gainst all these.

Lup. Innocence! O impudence! let me see, let me see! Is not here an eagle! and is not that eagle meant by Caesar, ha? Does not Caesar give the eagle? answer me; what sayest thou?

Tuc. Hast thou any evasion, stinkard?

Lup. Now he's turn'd dumb. I'll tickle you, Satyr.

Hor. Pish: ha, ha!

Lup. Dost thou pish me? Give me my long sword.

Hor.
  With reverence to great Caesar, worthy Romans,
  Observe but this ridiculous commenter;
  The soul 'to my device was in this distich:
  Thus oft, the base and ravenous multitude
  Survive, to share the spoils of fortitude.
  Which in this body I have figured here,
  A vulture--

Lup. A vulture! Ay, now, 'tis a vulture. O abominable! monstrous! monstrous! has not your vulture a beak? has it not legs, and talons, and wings, and feathers?

Tuc. Touch him, old buskins.

Hor. And therefore must it be an eagle?

Mec. Respect him not, good Horace: say your device.

Hor. A vulture and a wolf

Lup. A wolf! good: that's I; I am the wolf: my name's Lupus; I am meant by the wolf. On, on; a vulture and a wolf

Hor. Preying upon the carcass of an ass--

Lup. An ass! good still: that's I too; I am the ass. You mean me by the ass.

Mec. Prithee, leave braying then.

Hor. If you will needs take it, I cannot with modesty give it from you.

Mec.
  But, by that beast, the old Egyptians
  Were wont to figure, in their hieroglyphics,
  Patience, frugality, and fortitude;
  For none of which we can suspect you, tribune.

Caes. Who was it, Lupus, that inform'd you first, This should be meant by us? Or was't your comment?

Lup. No, Caesar; a player gave me the first light of it indeed.

Tuc. Ay, an honest sycophant-like slave, and a politician besides

Caes. Where is that player?

Tuc. He is without here.

Caes. Call him in.

Tuc. Call in the player there: master AEsop, call him.

Equites. [within.] Player! where is the player? bear back: none but the player enter.
       [Enter AESOP, followed by CRISPINUS and DEMETRIUS.
Tuc. Yes, this gentleman and his Achates must.

Cris. Pray you, master usher:--we'll stand close, here.

Tuc. 'Tis a gentleman of quality, this; though he be somewhat out of clothes, I tell ye.--Come, AEsop, hast a bay leaf in thy mouth? Well said; be not out, stinkard. Thou shalt have a monopoly of playing confirm'd to thee, and thy covey, under the emperor's broad seal, for this service.

Caes. Is this he?

Lup. Ay, Caesar, this is he.

Caes.
  Let him be whipped. Lictors, go take him hence.
  And, Lupus, for your fierce credulity,
  One fit him with a pair of larger ears:
  'Tis Caesar's doom, and must not be revoked.
  We hate to have our court and peace disturb'd
  With these quotidian clamours. See it done.

Lup. Caesar! [Exeunt some of the Lictors, with Lupus and AEsop

Caes. Gag him, [that] we may have his silence.

Virg.
>   Caesar hath done like Caesar. Fair and just
>   Is his award, against these brainless creatures.
>   'Tis not the wholesome sharp morality,
>   Or modest anger of a satiric spirit,
>   That hurts or wounds the body of the state;
>   But the sinister application
>   Of the malicious, ignorant, and base
>   Interpreter; who will distort, and strain
>   The general scope and purpose of an author
>   To his particular and private spleen.

Caes.
>   We know it, our dear Virgil, and esteem it
>   A most dishonest practice in that man,
>   Will seem too witty in another's work.
>   What would Cornelius Gallus, and Tibullus?
>   [They whisper Caesar.

Tuc. [to Mecaenas.] Nay, but as thou art a man, dost hear! a man of worship and honourable: hold, here, take thy chain again. Resume, mad Mecoenas. What! dost thou think I meant to have kept it, old boy? no: I did it but to fright thee, I, to try how thou would'st take it. What! will I turn shark upon my friends, or my friends' friends? I scorn it with my three souls. Come, I love bully Horace as well as thou dost, I: 'tis an honest hieroglyphic. Give me thy wrist, Helicon. Dost thou think I'll second e'er a rhinoceros of them all, against thee, ha? or thy noble Hippocrene, here? I'll turn stager first, and be whipt too: dost thou see, bully?

Caes.
>   You have your will of Caesar: use it, Romans.
>   Virgil shall be your praetor: and ourself

Will here sit by, spectator of your sports;
And think it no impeach of royalty.
Our ear is now too much profaned, grave Maro,
With these distastes, to take thy sacred lines;
Put up thy book, till both the time and we
Be fitted with more hallow'd circumstance
For the receiving of so divine a work.
Proceed with your design.

Mec. Gal. Tib. Thanks to great Caesar.

Gal. Tibullus, draw you the indictment then, whilst Horace arrests them on the statute of Calumny. Mecaenas and I will take our places here. Lictors, assist him.

Hor. I am the worst accuser under heaven.

Gal. Tut, you must do it; 'twill be noble mirth.

Hor. I take no knowledge that they do malign me.

Tib. Ay, but the world takes knowledge.

Hor.
   Would the world knew
   How heartily I wish a fool should hate me!

Tuc. Body of Jupiter! what! will they arraign my brisk Poetaster and his poor journeyman, ha? Would I were abroad skeldering for, a drachm, so I were out of this labyrinth again! I do feel myself turn stinkard already: but I must set the best face I have upon't now. [Aside.]--Well said, my divine, deft Horace, bring the whoreson detracting slaves to the bar, do; make them hold up their spread golls: I'll give in evidence for thee, if thou wilt. Take courage, Crispinus; would thy man had a clean band!

Cris. What must we do, captain?

Tuc. Thou shalt see anon: do not make division with thy legs so.

Caes. What's he, Horace?

Hor. I only know him for a motion, Caesar.

Tuc. I am one of thy commanders, Caesar; a man of service and action: my name is Pantilius Tucca; I have served in thy wars against Mark Antony, I.

Caes. Do you know him, Cornelius?

Gal. He's one that hath had the mustering, or convoy of a company now and then: I never noted him by any other employment.

Caes. We will observe him better.

Tib. Lictor, proclaim silence in the court.

Lict. In the name of Caesar, silence!

Tib. Let the parties, the accuser and the accused, present themselves.

Lict. The accuser and the accused, present yourselves in court.

Cris. Dem. Here.

Virg. Read the indictment.

Tib. Rufus Laberius Crispinus, and Demetrius Fannius, hold up your hands. You are, before this time, jointly and severally indicted, and here presently to be arraigned upon the statute of calumny, or Lex Remmia, the one by the name of Rufus Laberius Crispinus, alias Cri-spinus, poetaster and plagiary, the other by the name of Demetrius Fannius, play-dresser and plagiary. That you (not having the fear of Phoebus, or his shafts, before your eyes) contrary to the peace of our liege lord, Augustus Caesar, his crown and dignity, and against the form of a statute, in that case made and provided, have moat ignorantly, foolishly, and, more like yourselves, maliciously, gone about to deprave, and calumniate the person and writings of Quintus Horatius Flaccus, here present, poet, and priest to the Muses, and to that end have mutually conspired and plotted, at sundry times, as by several means, and in sundry places, for the better accomplishing your base and envious purpose, taxing him falsely, of self-love, arrogancy, impudence, railing, filching by translation, etc. Of all which calumnies, and every of them, in manner and form aforesaid, what answer you! Are you guilty, or not guilty?

Tuc. Not guilty, say.

Cris. Dem. Not guilty.

Tib. How will you be tried ?
                    [Aside to Crispinus.
Tuc. By the Roman Gods, and the noblest Romans.

Cris. Dem. By the Roman gods, and the noblest Romans.

Virg. Here sits Mecaenas, and Cornelius Gallus, are you contented

to be tried by these?
                              [Aside.
Tuc. Ay, so the noble captain may be joined with them in commission, say.

Cris. Dem. Ay, so the noble captain may be joined with them in commission.

Virg. What says the plaintiff?

Hor. I am content.

Virg. Captain, then take your place.

Tuc. alas, my worshipful praetor! 'tis more of thy gentleness than of my deserving, I wusse. But since it hath pleased the court to make choice of my wisdom and gravity, come, my calumnious varlets; let's hear you talk for yourselves, now, an hour or two. What can you say? Make a noise. Act, act!

Virg.
  Stay, turn, and take an oath first. You shall swear,
  By thunder-darting Jove, the king of gods,
  And by the genius of Augustus Caesar;
  By your own white and uncorrupted souls,
  And the deep reverence of our Roman justice;
  To judge this case, with truth and equity:
  As bound by your religion, and your laws.
  Now read the evidence: but first demand
  Of either prisoner, if that writ be theirs.
                              [Gives him two papers.
Tib. Shew this unto Crispinus. Is it yours?

Tuc. Say, ay. [Aside.]--What! dost thou stand upon it, pimp! Do not deny thine own Minerva, thy Pallas, the issue of thy brain.

Oris. Yes it is mine.

Tib. Shew that unto Demetrius. Is it yours?

Dem. It is.

Tuc. There's a father will not deny his own bastard now, I warrant thee.

Virg. Read them aloud.

Tib.
  Ramp up my genius, be not retrograde;
  But boldly nominate a spade a spade
  What, shall thy lubrical and glibbery muse
  Live, as she were defunct, like punk in stews!

Tuc. Excellent!

  Alas! that were no modern consequence,
  To have cothurnal buskins frighted hence.
  No, teach thy Incubus to poetise;
  And throw abroad thy spurious snotteries,
  Upon that puft-up lump of balmy froth,

Tuc. Ah, Ah!

  Or clumsy chilblain'd judgment; that with oath
  Magnificates his merit; and beapawls
  The conscious time, with humorous foam and brawls,

>   As if his organons of sense would crack
>   The sinews of my patience. Break his back,
>   O poets all and some! for now we list
>   Of strenuous vengeance to clutch the fist.
>   CRISPINUS.

Tuc. Ay, marry, this was written like a Hercules in poetry, now.

Caes. Excellently well threaten'd!

Virg. And as strangely worded, Caesar.

Caes. We observe it.

Virg. The other now.

Tuc. This is a fellow of a good prodigal tongue too, this will do well.

Tib.
>   Our Muse is in mind for th' untrussing a poet,
>   I slip by his name, for most men do know it:
>   A critic, that all the world bescumbers
>   With satirical humours and lyrical numbers:

Tuc. Art thou there, boy?

>   And for the most part, himself doth advance
>   With much self-love, and more arrogance.

Tuc. Good again!

>   And, but that I would not be thought a prater,

I could tell you he were a translator.
　　I know the authors from whence he has stole,
　　And could trace him too, but that
　　I understand them not full and whole.

Tuc. That line is broke loose from all his fellows: chain him up shorter, do.

　　The best note I can give you to know him by,
　　Is, that he keeps gallants' company;
　　Whom I could wish, in time should him fear,
　　Lest after they buy repentance too dear.
　　　　　DEME. FANNIUS.

Tuc. Well said! This carries palm with it.

Hor.
　　And why, thou motley gull, why should they fear!
　　When hast thou known us wrong or tax a friend?
　　I dare thy malice to betray it. Speak.
　　Now thou curl'st up, thou poor and nasty snake,
　　And shrink'st thy poisonous head into thy bosom:
　　Out, viper! thou that eat'st thy parents, hence!
　　Rather, such speckled creatures, as thyself,
　　Should be eschew'd, and shunn'd; such as will bite
　　And gnaw their absent friends, not cure their fame;
　　Catch at the loosest laughters, and affect
　　To be thought jesters; such as can devise
　　Things never seen, or head, t'impair men's names,
　　And gratify their credulous adversaries;
　　Will carry tales, do basest offices,
　　Cherish divided fires, and still encrease
　　New flames, out of old embers; will reveal

Each secret that's committed to their trust:
These be black slaves; Romans, take heed of these.

Tuc. Thou twang'st right, little Horace: they be indeed a couple of chap-fall'n curs. Come, we of the bench, let's rise to the urn, and condemn them quickly.

Virg.
  Before you go together, worthy Romans,
  We are to tender our opinion;
  And give you those instructions, that may add
  Unto your even judgment in the cause:
  Which thus we do commence. First, you must know,
  That where there is a true and perfect merit,
  There can be no dejection; and the scorn
  Of humble baseness, oftentimes so works
  In a high soul, upon the grosser spirit,
  That to his bleared and offended sense,
  There seems a hideous fault blazed in the object;
  When only the disease is in his eyes.
  Here-hence it comes our Horace now stands tax'd
  Of impudence, self-love, and arrogance,
  By those who share no merit in themselves;
  And therefore think his portion is as small.
  For they, from their own guilt, assure their souls,
  If they should confidently praise their works,
  In them it would appear inflation:
  Which, in a full and well digested man,
  Cannot receive that foul abusive name,
  But the fair title of erection.
  And, for his true use of translating men,
  It still hath been a work of as much palm,
  In clearest judgments, as to invent or make,

His sharpness,---that is most excusable;
As being forced out of a suffering virtue,
Oppressed with the license of the time:---
And howsoever fools or jerking pedants,
Players, or suchlike buffoon barking wits,
May with their beggarly and barren trash
Tickle base vulgar ears, in their despite;
This, like Jove's thunder, shall their pride control,
"The honest satire hath the happiest soul."

Now, Romans, you have heard our thoughts;
  withdraw when you please.

Tib. Remove the accused from the bar.

Tuc. Who holds the urn to us, ha? Fear nothing, I'll quit you, mine honest pitiful stinkards; I'll do't.

Cris. Captain, you shall eternally girt me to you, as I am generous.

Tuc. Go to.

Caes. Tibullus, let there be a case of vizards privately provided; we have found a subject to bestow them on.

Tib. It shall be done, Caesar.

Caes. Here be words, Horace, able to bastinado a man's ears.

Hor. Ay.
  Please it, great Caesar, I have pills about me,
  Mixt with the whitest kind of hellebore,

Would give him a light vomit, that should purge
His brain and stomach of those tumorous heats:
Might I have leave to minister unto him.

Caes.
O, be his AEsculapius, gentle Horace!
You shall have leave, and he shall be your patient. Virgil,
Use your authority, command him forth.

Virg.
Caesar is careful of your health, Crispinus;
And hath himself chose a physician
To minister unto you: take his pills.

Hor.
They are somewhat bitter, sir, but very wholesome.
Take yet another; so: stand by, they'll work anon.

Tib. Romans, return to your several seats: lictors, bring forward
the urn; and set the accused to the bar.

Tuc. Quickly, you whoreson egregious varlets; come forward. What!
shall we sit all day upon you? You make no more haste now, than a
beggar upon pattens; or a physician to a patient that has no money,
you pilchers.

Tib. Rufus Laberius Crispinus, and Demetrius Fannius, hold up your
hands. You have, according to the Roman custom, put yourselves upon
trial to the urn, for divers and sundry calumnies, whereof you
have, before this time, been indicted, and are now presently
arraigned: prepare yourselves to hearken to the verdict of your
tryers. Caius Cilnius Mecaenas pronounceth you, by this
hand-writing, guilty. Cornelius Gallus, guilty. Pantilius Tucca--

Tuc. Parcel-guilty, I.

Dem.
  He means himself; for it was he indeed
  Suborn'd us to the calumny.

Tuc. I, you whoreson cantharides! was it I?

Dem. I appeal to your conscience, captain.

Tib. Then you confess it now?

Dem. I do, and crave the mercy of the court.

Tib. What saith Crispinus?

Cris. O, the captain, the captain---

Bor. My physic begins to work with my patient, I see.

Virg. Captain, stand forth and answer.

Tuc. Hold thy peace, poet praetor: I appeal from thee to Caesar, I.
Do me right, royal Caesar.

Caes.
  Marry, and I will, sir.---Lictors, gag him; do.
  And put a case of vizards o'er his head,
  That he may look bifronted, as he speaks.

Tuc. Gods and fiends! Caesar! thou wilt not, Caesar, wilt thou?
Away, you whoreson vultures; away. You think I am a dead corps now,
because Caesar is disposed to jest with a man of mark, or so. Hold

your hook'd talons out of my flesh, you inhuman harpies. Go to, do't. What! will the royal Augustus cast away a gentleman of worship, a captain and a commander, for a couple of condemn'd caitiff calumnious cargos?

Caes. Dispatch, lictors.

Tuc. Caesar!　　　　　[The vizards are put upon him.

Caes. Forward, Tibullus.

Virg. Demand what cause they had to malign Horace.

Dem. In troth, no great cause, not I, I must confess; but that he kept better company, for the most part, than I; and that better men loved him than loved me; and that his writings thrived better than mine, and were better liked and graced: nothing else.

Virg.
　Thus envious souls repine at others' good.

Hor.
　If this be all, faith, I forgive thee freely.
　Envy me still, so long as Virgil loves me,
　Gallus, Tibullus, and the best-best Caesar,
　My dear Mecaenas; while these, with many more,
　Whose names I wisely slip, shall think me worthy
　Their honour'd and adored society,
　And read and love, prove and applaud my poems;
　I would not wish but such as you should spite them.

Cris. O--!

Tib. How now, Crispinus? C

Cris. O, I am sick--!

Hor. A bason, a bason, quickly; our physic works. Faint not, man.

Cris. O------retrograde------reciprocal------incubus.

Caes. What's that, Horace?

Hor. Retrograde, reciprocal, and incubus, are come up.

Gal. Thanks be to Jupiter!

Cris. O------glibbery------lubrical------defunct------O------!

Hor. Well said; here's some store.

Virg. What are they?

Hor. Glibbery, lubrical, and defunct.

Gal. O, they came up easy.

Cris. O------O------!

Tib. What's that?

Hor. Nothing yet.

Cris. Magnificate------

Mec. Magnificate! That came up somewhat hard.

Hor. Ay. What cheer, Crispinus?

Cris. O! I shall cast up my------spurious------snotteries------

Hor. Good. Again.

Oris. Chilblain'd------O------O------clumsie------

Hor. That clumsie stuck terribly.

Mec. What's all that, Horace?

Hor. Spurious, snotteries, chilblain'd, clumsie.

Tib. O Jupiter!

Gal. Who would have thought there should have been such a deal of filth in a poet?

Cris. O------balmy froth------

Caes. What's that?

Cris.------Puffie------inflate------turgidious-------ventosity.

Hor. Balmy, froth, puffie, inflate, turgidous, and ventosity are come up.

Tib. O terrible windy words.

Gal. A sign of a windy brain.

Cris. O------oblatrant------furibund------fatuate------strenuous---

Hor. Here's a deal; oblatrant, furibund, fatuate, strenuous.

Caes. Now all's come up, I trow. What a tumult he had in his belly?

Hor. No, there's the often conscious damp behind still.

Cris. O------conscious------damp.

Hor. It is come up, thanks to Apollo and AEsculapius: another; you were best take a pill more.

Cris. O, no; O------O------O------O------O!

Hor. Force yourself then a little with your finger.

Cris. O------O------prorumped.

Tib. Prorumped I What a noise it made! as if his spirit would have prorumpt with it.

Cris. O------O------O !

Virg. Help him, it sticks strangely, whatever it is.

Cris. O------clutcht

Hor. Now it is come; clutcht.

Caes. Clutcht! it is well that's come up; it had but a narrow passage.

Cris. O------!

Virg. Again! hold him, hold his head there.

Cris. Snarling gusts------quaking custard.

Hor. How now, Crispinus?

Cris. O------obstupefact.

Tib. Nay, that are all we, I assure you.

Hor. How do you feel yourself?

Cris. Pretty and well, I thank you.

Virg.
  These pills can but restore him for a time,
  Not cure him quite of such a malady,
  Caught by so many surfeits, which have fill'd
  His blood and brain thus full of crudities:
  'Tis necessary therefore he observe
  A strict and wholesome diet. Look you take
  Each morning of old Cato's principles
  A good draught next your heart; that walk upon,
  Till it be well digested: then come home,
  And taste a piece of Terence, suck his phrase
  Instead of liquorice; and, at any hand,
  Shun Plautus and old Ennius: they are meats
  Too harsh for a weak stomach.
  Use to read (But not without a tutor) the best Greeks,
  As Orpheus, Musaeus, Pindarus,
  Hesiod, Callimachus, and Theocrite,
  High Homer; but beware of Lycophron,
  He is too dark and dangerous a dish.

You must not hunt for wild outlandish terms,
To stuff out a peculiar dialect;
But let your matter run before your words.
And if at any time you chance to meet
Some Gallo-Belgic phrase; you shall not straight.
Rack your poor verse to give it entertainment,
But let it pass; and do not think yourself
Much damnified, if you do leave it out,
When nor your understanding, nor the sense
Could well receive it. This fair abstinence,
In time, will render you more sound and clear:
And this have I prescribed to you, in place
Of a strict sentence; which till he perform,
Attire him in that robe. And henceforth learn
To bear yourself more humbly; not to swell,
Or breathe your insolent and idle spite
On him whose laughter can your worst affright.

Tib. Take him away.

Cris. Jupiter guard Caesar!

Virg.
  And for a week or two see him lock'd up
In some dark place, removed from company;
He will talk idly else after his physic.
Now to you, sir. [to Demetrius.] The extremity of law
Awards you to be branded in the front,
For this your calumny; but since it pleaseth
Horace, the party wrong'd, t' intreat of Caesar
A mitigation of that juster doom,
With Caesar's tongue thus we pronounce your sentence.
Demetrius Fannius, thou shalt here put on

That coat and cap, and henceforth think thyself
No other than they make thee; vow to wear them
In every fair and generous assembly,
Till the best sort of minds shall take to knowledge
As well thy satisfaction, as thy wrongs.

Hor.
Only, grave praetor, here, in open court,
I crave the oath for good behaviour
May be administer'd unto them both.

Virg.
Horace, it shall: Tibullus, give it them.

Tib. Rufus Laberius Crispinus, and Demetrius Fannius, lay your hands on your hearts. You shall here solemnly attest and swear, that never, after this instant, either at booksellers' stalls, in taverns, two-penny rooms, tyring-houses, noblemen's butteries, puisents chambers, (the best and farthest places where you are admitted to come,) you shall once offer or dare (thereby to endear yourself the more to any player, enghle, or guilty gull in your company) to malign, traduce, or detract the person or writings of Quintus Horatius Flaccus, or any other eminent men, transcending you in merit, whom your envy shall find cause to work upon, either for that, or for keeping himself in better acquaintance, or enjoying better friends, or if, transported by any sudden and desperate resolution, you do, that then you shall not under the batoon, or in the next presence, being an honourable assembly of his favourers, be brought as voluntary gentlemen to undertake the for-swearing of it. Neither shall you, at any time, ambitiously affecting the title of the Untrussers or Whippers of the age, suffer the itch of writing to over-run your performance in libel, upon pain of being taken up for lepers in wit, and, losing both your time and your papers, be irrecoverably forfeited to the hospital of fools. So help you our Roman gods and the Genius of great Caesar.

Virg. So! now dissolve the court.

Bor. Tib. Gal. Mec. And thanks to Caesar, That thus hath exercised his patience.

Caes.
  We have, indeed, you worthiest friends of Caesar.
  It is the bane and torment of our ears,
  To hear the discords of those jangling rhymers,
  That with their bad and scandalous practices
  Bring all true arts and learning in contempt.
  But let not your high thoughts descend so low
  As these despised objects; let them fall,
  With their flat grovelling souls: be you yourselves;
  And as with our best favours you stand crown'd,
  So let your mutual loves be still renown'd.
  Envy will dwell where there is want of merit,
  Though the deserving man should crack his spirit.

    Blush, folly, blush; here's none that fears
    The wagging of an ass's ears,
    Although a wolfish case he wears.
    Detraction is but baseness' varlet;
    And apes are apes, though clothed in scarlet.   [*Exeunt.*

    Rumpatur, quisquis rumpitur invidi!

"Here, reader, in place of the epilogue, was meant to thee an apology from the author, with his reasons for the publishing of this book: but, since he is no less restrained than thou deprived of it by authority, he prays thee to think charitably of what thou hast read. till thou mayest hear him speak what he hath written."

HORACE AND TREBATIUS.
A DIALOGUE.
Sat. 1. Lib. 2.

Hor.
    There are to whom I seem excessive sour,
    And past a satire's law t' extend my power:
    Others, that think whatever I have writ
    Wants pith and matter to eternise it;
    And that they could, in one day's light, disclose
    A thousand verses, such as I compose.
    What shall I do, Trebatius? say.

Treb. Surcease.

Hor. And shall my muse admit no more increase?

Treb. So I advise.

Hor.
    An ill death let me die,
    If 'twere not best; but sleep avoids mine eye,
    And I use these, lest nights should tedious seem.

Treb.
  Rather, contend to sleep, and live like them,
  That, holding golden sleep in special price,
  Rubb'd with sweet oils, swim silver Tyber thrice,
  And every even with neat wine steeped be:
  Or, if such love of writing ravish thee,
  Then dare to sing unconquer'd Caesar's deeds;
  Who cheers such actions with abundant meeds.

Hor.
  That, father, I desire; but, when I try,
  I feel defects in every faculty:
  Nor is't a labour fit for every pen,
  To paint the horrid troops of armed men,
  The lances burst, in Gallia's slaughter'd forces;
  Or wounded Parthians, tumbled from their horses:
  Great Caesar's wars cannot be fought with words.

Treb.
  Yet, what his virtue in his peace affords,
  His fortitude and justice thou canst shew
  As wise Lucilius honour'd Scipio.

Hor.
  Of that, my powers shall suffer no neglect,
  When such slight labours may aspire respect:
  But, if I watch not a most chosen time,
  The humble words of Flaccus cannot climb
  Th' attentive ear of Caesar; nor must I
  With less observance shun gross flattery:
  For he, reposed safe in his own merit,
  Spurns back the gloses of a fawning spirit.

Treb.
    But how much better would such accents sound
    Than with a sad and serious verse to wound
    Pantolabus, railing in his saucy jests,
    Or Nomentanus spent in riotous feasts?
    In satires, each man, though untouch'd, complains
    As he were hurt; and hates such biting strains.

Hor.
    What shall I do? Milonius shakes his heels
    In ceaseless dances, when his brain once feels
    The stirring fervour of the wine ascend;
    And that his eyes false numbers apprehend.
    Castor his horse, Pollux loves handy-fights;
    A thousand heads, a thousand choice delights.
    My pleasure is in feet my words to close,
    As, both our better, old Lucilius does:
    He, as his trusty friends, his books did trust
    With all his secrets; nor, in things unjust,
    Or actions lawful, ran to other men:
    So that the old man's life described, was seen
    As in a votive table in his lines:
    And to his steps my genius inclines;
    Lucanian, or Apulian, I know not whether,
    For the Venusian colony ploughs either;
    Sent thither, when the Sabines were forced thence,
    As old Fame sings, to give the place defence
    'Gainst such as, seeing it empty, might make road
    Upon the empire; or there fix abode:
    Whether the Apulian borderer it were,
    Or the Lucanian violence they fear.---
    But this my style no living man shall touch,
    If first I be not forced by base reproach;

But like a sheathed sword it shall defend
My innocent life; for why should I contend
To draw it out, when no malicious thief
Robs my good name, the treasure of my life?
O Jupiter, let it with rust be eaten,
Before it touch, or insolently threaten
The life of any with the least disease;
So much I love, and woo a general peace.
But, he that wrongs me, better, I proclaim,
He never had assay'd to touch my fame.
For he shall weep, and walk with every tongue
Throughout the city, infamously sung.
Servius the praetor threats the laws, and urn,
If any at his deeds repine or spurn;
The witch Canidia, that Albutius got,
Denounceth witchcraft, where she loveth not;
Thurius the judge, doth thunder worlds of ill,
To such as strive with his judicial will.
All men affright their foes in what they may,
Nature commands it, and men must obey.
Observe with me: The wolf his tooth doth use,
The bull his horn; and who doth this infuse,
But nature? There's luxurious Scaeva; trust
His long-lived mother with him; his so just
And scrupulous right-hand no mischief will;
No more than with his heel a wolf will kill,
Or ox with jaw: marry, let him alone
With temper'd poison to remove the croan.
But briefly, if to age I destined be,
Or that quick death's black wings environ me;
If rich, or poor; at Rome; or fate command
I shall be banished to some other land;
What hue soever my whole state shall bear,

    I will write satires still, in spite of fear.

Treb.
    Horace, I fear thou draw'st no lasting breath;
    And that some great man's friend will be thy death.

Hor.
    What! when the man that first did satirise
    Durst pull the skin over the ears of vice,
    And make who stood in outward fashion clear,
    Give place, as foul within; shall I forbear?
    Did Laelius, or the man so great with fame,
    That from sack'd Carthage fetch'd his worthy name,
    Storm that Lucilius did Metellus pierce,
    Or bury Lupus quick in famous verse?
    Rulers and subjects, by whole tribes he checkt,
    But virtue and her friends did still protect:
    And when from sight, or from the judgment-seat,
    The virtuous Scipio and wise Laelius met,
    Unbraced, with him in all light sports they shared,
    Till their most frugal suppers were prepared.
    Whate'er I am, though both for wealth and wit
    Beneath Lucilius I am pleased to sit;
    Yet Envy, spite of her empoison'd breast,
    Shall say, I lived in grace here with the best;
    And seeking in weak trash to make her wound,
    Shall find me solid, and her teeth unsound:
    'Less learn'd Trebatius' censure disagree.

Treb.
    No, Horace, I of force must yield to thee;
    Only take heed, as being advised by me,
    Lest thou incur some danger: better pause,

Than rue thy ignorance of the sacred laws;
There's justice, and great action may be sued
'Gainst such as wrong men's fames with verses lewd.

Hor.
Ay, with lewd verses, such as libels be,
And aim'd at persons of good quality:
I reverence and adore that just decree.
But if they shall be sharp, yet modest rhymes,
That spare men's persons, and but tax their crimes,
Such shall in open court find current pass,
Were Caesar judge, and with the maker's grace.

Treb.
Nay, I'll add more; if thou thyself, being clear,
Shall tax in person a man fit to bear
Shame and reproach, his suit shall quickly be
Dissolved in laughter, and thou thence set free.

TO THE READER

If, by looking on what is past, thou hast deserved that name, I am willing thou should'st yet know more, by that which follows, an APOLOGETICAL DIALOGUE; which was only once spoken upon the stage and all the answer I ever gave to sundry impotent libels then cast out (and some yet remaining) against me, and this play. Wherein I take no pleasure to revive the times; but that posterity may make a difference between their manners that provoked me then, and mine that neglected them ever, For, in these strifes, and on such persons, were as wretched to affect a victory, as it is unhappy to be committed with them.

Non annorum canities est laudanda, sed morum.

SCENE, The Author's Lodgings.
Enter NASUTUS and POLYPOSUS.

Nas. I pray You let's go see him, how he looks
After these libels.

Pol. O vex'd, vex'd, I warrant you.

Nas. Do you think so? I should be sorry for him,
If I found that.

Pol. O, they are such bitter things,
He cannot choose.

Nas. But, is he guilty of them?

Pol. Fuh! that's no matter.

Nas. No !

Pol. No. Here's his lodging.
We'll steal upon him: or let's listen; stay.
He has a humour oft to talk t' himself.

Nas. They are your manners lead me, not mine own.
    [They come forward; the scene opens, and discovers the
      Author in his study.

Aut.
>The fates have not spun him the coarsest thread,
>That (free from knots of perturbation)
>Doth yet so live, although but to himself,
>As he can safely scorn the tongues of slaves,
>And neglect fortune, more than she can him.
>It is the happiest thing this, not to be
>Within the reach of malice; it provides
>A man so well, to laugh off injuries;
>And never sends him farther for his vengeance,
>Than the vex'd bosom of his enemy.
>I, now, but think how poor their spite sets off,
>Who, after all their waste of sulphurous terms,
>And burst-out thunder of their charged mouths,
>Have nothing left but the unsavoury smoke
>Of their black vomit, to upbraid themselves:
>Whilst I, at whom they shot, sit here shot-free,
>And as unhurt of envy, as unhit.
>>[Pol. and Nas. discover themselves.

Pol.
>Ay, but the multitude they think not so, sir,
>They think you hit, and hurt: and dare give out,
>Your silence argues it in not rejoining
>To this or that late libel.

Aut.
>'Las, good rout!
>I can afford them leave to err so still;
>And like the barking students of Bears-college,
>To swallow up the garbage of the time
>With greedy gullets, whilst myself sit by,
>Pleased, and yet tortured, with their beastly feeding.

'Tis a sweet madness runs along with them,
To think, all that are aim'd at still are struck:
Then, where the shaft still lights, make that the mark:
And so each fear or fever-shaken fool
May challenge Teucer's hand in archery.
Good troth, if I knew any man so vile,
To act the crimes these Whippers reprehend,
Or what their servile apes gesticulate,
I should not then much muse their shreds were liked;
Since ill men have a lust t' hear others' sins,
All good men have a zeal to hear sin shamed.
But when it is all excrement they vent,
Base filth and offal; or thefts, notable
As ocean-piracies, or highway-stands;
And not a crime there tax'd, but is their own,
Or what their own foul thoughts suggested to them;
And that, in all their heat of taxing others,
Not one of them but lives himself, if known,
Improbior satiram scribente cinaedo
What should I say more, than turn stone with wonder!

Nas.
I never saw this play bred all this tumult:
What was there in it could so deeply offend
And stir so many hornets?

Aut. Shall I tell you?

Nas. Yea, and ingeniouosly.

Aut.
Then, by the hope
Which I prefer unto all other objects,

I can profess, I never writ that piece
More innocent or empty of offence.
Some salt it had, but neither tooth nor gall,
Nor was there in it any circumstance
Which. in the setting down, I could suspect
Might be perverted by an enemy's tongue;
Only it had the fault to be call'd mine;
That was the crime.

Pol.
  No! why, they say you tax'd
The law and lawyers, captains and the players,
By their particular names.

Aut. It is not so.
  I used no name. My books have still been taught
To spare the persons, and to speak the vices.
These are mere slanders, and enforced by such
As have no safer ways to men's disgraces.
But their own lies and loss of honesty:
Fellows of practised and most laxative tongues,
Whose empty and eager bellies, in the year,
Compel their brains to many desperate shifts,
(I spare to name them, for their wretchedness
Fury itself would pardon). These, or such,
Whether of malice, or of ignorance,
Or itch t' have me their adversary, I know not,
Or all these mixt; but sure I am, three years
They did provoke me with their petulant styles
On every stage: and I at last unwilling,
But weary, I confess, of so much trouble,
Thought I would try if shame could win upon 'em,'
And therefore chose Augustus Caesar's times,

When wit and area were at their height in Rome,
To shew that Virgil, Horace, and the rest
Of those great master-spirits, did not want
Detractors then, or practicers against them:
And by this line, although no parallel,
I hoped at last they would sit down and blush;
But nothing I could find more contrary.
And though the impudence of flies be great,
Yet this hath so provok'd the angry wasps,
Or, as you said, of the next nest, the hornets,
That they fly buzzing, mad, about my nostrils,
And, like so many screaming grasshoppers
Held by the wings, fill every ear with noise.
And what? those former calumnies you mention'd.
First, of the law: indeed I brought in Ovid
Chid by his angry father for neglecting
The study of their laws for poetry:
And I am warranted by his own words:

    Saepe pater dixit, studium quid inutile tentas!
        Maeonides nullas ipse reliquit opes.

And in far harsher terms elsewhere, as these:

    Non me verbosas leges ediscere, non me
        Ingrato voces prostituisse foro.

But how this should relate unto our laws,
Or the just ministers, with least abuse,
I reverence both too much to understand!
Then, for the captain, I will only speak
An epigram I here have made: it is

UNTO TRUE SOLDIERS.
        That's the lemma: mark it.
Strength of my country, whilst I bring to view
Such: as are miss-call'd captains, and wrong you,
And your high names; I do desire, that thence,
Be nor put on you, nor you take offence:
I swear by your true friend, my muse, I love
Your great profession which I once did prove;
And did not shame it with my actions then,
No more than I dare now do with my pen.
He that not trusts me, having vowed thus much,
But's angry for the captain, still: is such.
Now for the players, it is true, I tax'd them,
And yet but some; and those so sparingly,
As all the rest might have sat still unquestion'd,
Had they but had the wit or conscience
To think well of themselves. But impotent, they
Thought each man's vice belong'd to their whole tribe;
And much good do't them! What they have done 'gainst me,
I am not moved with: if it gave them meat,
Or got them clothes, 'tis well; that was their end.
Only amongst them, I am sorry for
Some better natures, by the rest so drawn,
To run in that vile line.

Pol. And is this all!
Will you not answer then the libels?

Aut. No.

Pol. Nor the Untrussers?

Aut. Neither.

THE POETASTER OR HIS ARRAIGNMENT

Pol. Y'are undone then.

Aut. With whom?

Pol. The world.

Aut. The bawd!

Pol. It will be taken
  To be stupidity or tameness in you.

Aut.
  But they that have incensed me, can in soul
  Acquit me of that guilt. They know I dare
  To spurn or baffle them, or squirt their eyes
  With ink or urine; or I could do worse,
  Arm'd with Archilochus' fury, write Iambics,
  Should make the desperate lashers hang themselves;
  Rhime them to death, as they do Irish rats
  In drumming tunes. Or, living, I could stamp
  Their foreheads with those deep and public brands,
  That the whole company of barber-surgeon a
  Should not take off with all their art and plasters.
  And these my prints should last, still to be read
  In their pale fronts; when, what they write 'gainst me
  Shall, like a figure drawn in water, fleet,
  And the poor wretched papers be employed
  To clothe tobacco, or some cheaper drug:
  This I could do, and make them infamous.
  But, to what end? when their own deeds have mark'd 'em;
  And that I know, within his guilty breast
  Each slanderer bears a whip that shall torment him

    Worse than a million of these temporal plagues:
    Which to pursue, were but a feminine humour,
    And far beneath the dignity of man.

Nas.
    'Tis true; for to revenge their injuries,
    Were to confess you felt them. Let them go,
    And use the treasure of the fool, their tongues,
    Who makes his gain, by speaking worst of beat.

Pol. O, but they lay particular imputations--

Aut. As what?

Pol. That all your writing is mere railing.

Aut. Ha?
    If all the salt in the old comedy
    Should be so censured, or the sharper wit
    Of the bold satire termed scolding rage,
    What age could then compare with those for buffoons?
    What should be said of Aristophanes,
    Persius, or Juvenal, whose names we now
    So glorify in schools, at least pretend it?---
    Have they no other?

Pol.
    Yes; they say you are slow,
    And scarce bring forth a play a year.

Aut. 'Tis true.
    I would they could not say that I did that !
    There's all the joy that I take in their trade,

THE POETASTER OR HIS ARRAIGNMENT

Unless such scribes as these might be proscribed
Th' abused theatres. They would think it strange, now,
A man should take but colts-foot for one day,
And, between whiles, spit out a better poem
Than e'er the master of art, or giver of wit,
Their belly, made. Yet, this is possible,
If a free mind had but the patience,
To think so much together and so vile.
But that these base and beggarly conceits
Should carry it, by the multitude of voices,
Against the most abstracted work, opposed
To the stuff'd nostrils of the drunken rout!
O, this would make a learn'd and liberal soul
To rive his stained quill up to the back,
And damn his long-watch'd labours to the fire,
Things that were born when none but the still night
And his dumb candle, saw his pinching throes,
Were not his own free merit a more crown
Unto his travails than their reeling claps.
This 'tis that strikes me silent, seals my lips,
And apts me rather to sleep out my time,
Than I would waste it in contemned strifes
With these vile Ibides, these unclean birds,
That make their mouths their clysters, and still purge
From their hot entrails. But I leave the monsters
To their own fate. And, since the Comic Muse
Hath proved so ominous to me, I will try
If TRAGEDY have a more kind aspect;
Her favours in my next I will pursue,
Where, if I prove the pleasure but of one,
So he judicious be, he shall be alone
A theatre unto me; Once I'll say
To strike the ear of time in those fresh strains,

    As shall, beside the cunning of their ground,
Give cause to some of wonder, some despite,
  And more despair, to imitate their sound.
I, that spend half my nights, and all my days,
  Here in a cell, to get a dark paleface,
To come forth worth the ivy or the bays,
  And in this age can hope no other grace---
Leave me! There's something come into my thought,
That must and shall be sung high and aloof,
Safe from the wolfs black jaw, and the dun ass's hoof

Nas. I reverence these raptures, and obey them.
                        [The scene closes---

GLOSSARY

ABATE, cast down, subdue.

ABHORRING, repugnant (to), at variance.

ABJECT, base, degraded thing, outcast.

ABRASE, smooth, blank.

ABSOLUTE(LY), faultless(ly).

ABSTRACTED, abstract, abstruse.

ABUSE, deceive, insult, dishonour, make ill use of.

ACATER, caterer.

ACATES, cates.

ACCEPTIVE, willing, ready to accept, receive.

ACCOMMODATE, fit, befitting. (The word was a fashionable one and used on all occasions. See "Henry IV.," pt. 2, iii. 4).

ACCOST, draw near, approach.

ACKNOWN, confessedly acquainted with.

ACME, full maturity.

ADALANTADO, lord deputy or governor of a Spanish province.

ADJECTION, addition.

ADMIRATION, astonishment.

ADMIRE, wonder, wonder at.

ADROP, philosopher's stone, or substance from which obtained.

ADSCRIVE, subscribe.

ADULTERATE, spurious, counterfeit.

ADVANCE, lift.

ADVERTISE, inform, give intelligence.

ADVERTISED, "be--," be it known to you.

ADVERTISEMENT, intelligence.

ADVISE, consider, bethink oneself, deliberate.

ADVISED, informed, aware; "are you--?" have you found that out?

AFFECT, love, like; aim at; move.

AFFECTED, disposed; beloved.

AFFECTIONATE, obstinate; prejudiced.

AFFECTS, affections.

AFFRONT, "give the--," face.

AFFY, have confidence in; betroth.

AFTER, after the manner of.

AGAIN, AGAINST, in anticipation of.

AGGRAVATE, increase, magnify, enlarge upon.

AGNOMINATION. See Paranomasie.

AIERY, nest, brood.

AIM, guess.

ALL HID, children's cry at hide-and-seek.

ALL-TO, completely, entirely ("all-to-be-laden").

ALLOWANCE, approbation, recognition.

ALMA-CANTARAS (astronomy), parallels of altitude.

ALMAIN, name of a dance.

ALMUTEN, planet of chief influence in the horoscope.

ALONE, unequalled, without peer.

ALUDELS, subliming pots.

AMAZED, confused, perplexed.

AMBER, AMBRE, ambergris.

AMBREE, MARY, a woman noted for her valour at the siege of Ghent, 1458.

AMES-ACE, lowest throw at dice.

AMPHIBOLIES, ambiguities.

AMUSED, bewildered, amazed.

AN, if.

ANATOMY, skeleton, or dissected body.

ANDIRONS, fire-dogs.

ANGEL, gold coin worth 10 shillings, stamped with the figure of the archangel Michael.

ANNESH CLEARE, spring known as Agnes le Clare.

ANSWER, return hit in fencing.

ANTIC, ANTIQUE, clown, buffoon.

ANTIC, like a buffoon.

ANTIPERISTASIS, an opposition which enhances the quality it opposes.

APOZEM, decoction.

APPERIL, peril.

APPLE-JOHN, APPLE-SQUIRE, pimp, pander.

APPLY, attach.

APPREHEND, take into custody.

APPREHENSIVE, quick of perception; able to perceive and appreciate.

APPROVE, prove, confirm.

APT, suit, adapt; train, prepare; dispose, incline.

APT(LY), suitable(y), opportune(ly).

APTITUDE, suitableness.

ARBOR, "make the--," cut up the game (Gifford).

ARCHES, Court of Arches.

ARCHIE, Archibald Armstrong, jester to James I. and Charles I.

ARGAILE, argol, crust or sediment in wine casks.

ARGENT-VIVE, quicksilver.

ARGUMENT, plot of a drama; theme, subject; matter in question; token, proof.

ARRIDE, please.

ARSEDINE, mixture of copper and zinc, used as an imitation of gold-leaf.

ARTHUR, PRINCE, reference to an archery show by a society who assumed arms, etc., of Arthur's knights.

ARTICLE, item.

ARTIFICIALLY, artfully.

ASCENSION, evaporation, distillation.

ASPIRE, try to reach, obtain, long for.

ASSALTO (Italian), assault.

ASSAY, draw a knife along the belly of the deer, a ceremony of the hunting-field.

ASSOIL, solve.

ASSURE, secure possession or reversion of.

ATHANOR, a digesting furnace, calculated to keep up a constant heat.

ATONE, reconcile.

ATTACH, attack, seize.

AUDACIOUS, having spirit and confidence.

AUTHENTIC(AL), of authority, authorised, trustworthy, genuine.

AVISEMENT, reflection, consideration.

AVOID, begone! get rid of.

AWAY WITH, endure.

AZOCH, Mercurius Philosophorum.

BABION, baboon.

BABY, doll.

BACK-SIDE, back premises.

BAFFLE, treat with contempt.

BAGATINE, Italian coin, worth about the third of a farthing.

BAIARD, horse of magic powers known to old romance.

BALDRICK, belt worn across the breast to support bugle, etc.

BALE (of dice), pair.

BALK, overlook, pass by, avoid.

BALLACE, ballast.

BALLOO, game at ball.

BALNEUM (BAIN MARIE), a vessel for holding hot water in which other vessels are stood for heating.

BANBURY, "brother of--," Puritan.

BANDOG, dog tied or chained up.

BANE, woe, ruin.

BANQUET, a light repast; dessert.

BARB, to clip gold.

BARBEL, fresh-water fish.

BARE, meer; bareheaded; it was "a particular mark of state and grandeur for the coachman to be uncovered" (Gifford).

BARLEY-BREAK, game somewhat similar to base.

BASE, game of prisoner's base.

BASES, richly embroidered skirt reaching to the knees, or lower.

BASILISK, fabulous reptile, believed to slay with its eye.

BASKET, used for the broken provision collected for prisoners.

BASON, basons, etc., were beaten by the attendant mob when bad characters were "carted."

BATE, be reduced; abate, reduce.

BATOON, baton, stick.

BATTEN, feed, grow fat.

BAWSON, badger.

BEADSMAN, prayer-man, one engaged to pray for another.

BEAGLE, small hound; fig. spy.

BEAR IN HAND, keep in suspense, deceive with false hopes.

BEARWARD, bear leader.

BEDPHERE. See Phere.

BEDSTAFF, (?) wooden pin in the side of the bedstead for supporting the bedclothes (Johnson); one of the sticks or "laths"; a stick used in making a bed.

BEETLE, heavy mallet.

BEG, "I'd--him," the custody of minors and idiots was begged for; likewise property fallen forfeit to the Crown ("your house had been begged").

BELL-MAN, night watchman.

BENJAMIN, an aromatic gum.

BERLINA, pillory.

BESCUMBER, defile.

BESLAVE, beslabber.

BESOGNO, beggar.

BESPAWLE, bespatter.

BETHLEHEM GABOR, Transylvanian hero, proclaimed King of Hungary.

BEVER, drinking.

BEVIS, SIR, knight of romance whose horse was equally celebrated.

BEWRAY, reveal, make known.

BEZANT, heraldic term: small gold circle.

BEZOAR'S STONE, a remedy known by this name was a supposed antidote to poison.

BID-STAND, highwayman.

BIGGIN, cap, similar to that worn by the Beguines; nightcap.

BILIVE (belive), with haste.

BILK, nothing, empty talk.

BILL, kind of pike.

BILLET, wood cut for fuel, stick.

BIRDING, thieving.

BLACK SANCTUS, burlesque hymn, any unholy riot.

BLANK, originally a small French coin.

BLANK, white.

BLANKET, toss in a blanket.

BLAZE, outburst of violence.

BLAZE, (her.) blazon; publish abroad.

BLAZON, armorial bearings; fig. all that pertains to good birth and breeding.

BLIN, "withouten--," without ceasing.

BLOW, puff up.

BLUE, colour of servants' livery, hence "--order," "--waiters."

BLUSHET, blushing one.

BOB, jest, taunt.

BOB, beat, thump.

BODGE, measure.

BODKIN, dagger, or other short, pointed weapon; long pin with which the women fastened up their hair.

BOLT, roll (of material).

BOLT, dislodge, rout out; sift (boulting-tub).

BOLT'S-HEAD, long, straight-necked vessel for distillation.

BOMBARD SLOPS, padded, puffed-out breeches.

BONA ROBA, "good, wholesome, plum-cheeked wench" (Johnson) --not always used in compliment.

BONNY-CLABBER, sour butter-milk.

BOOKHOLDER, prompter.

BOOT, "to--," into the bargain; "no--," of no avail.

BORACHIO, bottle made of skin.

BORDELLO, brothel.

BORNE IT, conducted, carried it through.

BOTTLE (of hay), bundle, truss.

BOTTOM, skein or ball of thread; vessel.

BOURD, jest.

BOVOLI, snails or cockles dressed in the Italian manner (Gifford).

BOW-POT, flower vase or pot.

BOYS, "terrible--," "angry--," roystering young bucks. (See Nares).

BRABBLES (BRABBLESH), brawls.

BRACH, bitch.

BRADAMANTE, a heroine in "Orlando Furioso."

BRADLEY, ARTHUR OF, a lively character commemorated in ballads.

BRAKE, frame for confining a horse's feet while being shod, or strong curb or bridle; trap.

BRANCHED, with "detached sleeve ornaments, projecting from the shoulders of the gown" (Gifford).

BRANDISH, flourish of weapon.

BRASH, brace.

BRAVE, bravado, braggart speech.

BRAVE (adv.), gaily, finely (apparelled).

BRAVERIES, gallants.

BRAVERY, extravagant gaiety of apparel.

BRAVO, bravado, swaggerer.

BRAZEN-HEAD, speaking head made by Roger Bacon.

BREATHE, pause for relaxation; exercise.

BREATH UPON, speak dispraisingly of.

BREND, burn.

BRIDE-ALE, wedding feast.

BRIEF, abstract; (mus.) breve.

BRISK, smartly dressed.

BRIZE, breese, gadfly.

BROAD-SEAL, state seal.

BROCK, badger (term of contempt).

BROKE, transact business as a broker.

BROOK, endure, put up with.

BROUGHTON, HUGH, an English divine and Hebrew scholar.

BRUIT, rumour.

BUCK, wash.

BUCKLE, bend.

BUFF, leather made of buffalo skin, used for military and serjeants' coats, etc.

BUFO, black tincture.

BUGLE, long-shaped bead.

BULLED, (?) bolled, swelled.

BULLIONS, trunk hose.

BULLY, term of familiar endearment.

BUNGY, Friar Bungay, who had a familiar in the shape of a dog.

BURDEN, refrain, chorus.

BURGONET, closely-fitting helmet with visor.

BURGULLION, braggadocio.

BURN, mark wooden measures ("--ing of cans").

BURROUGH, pledge, security.

BUSKIN, half-boot, foot gear reaching high up the leg.

BUTT-SHAFT, barbless arrow for shooting at butts.

BUTTER, NATHANIEL ("Staple of News"), a compiler of general news. (See Cunningham).

BUTTERY-HATCH, half-door shutting off the buttery, where provisions and liquors were stored.

BUY, "he bought me," formerly the guardianship of wards could be bought.

BUZ, exclamation to enjoin silence.

BUZZARD, simpleton.

BY AND BY, at once.

BY(E), "on the ," incidentally, as of minor or secondary importance; at the side.

BY-CHOP, by-blow, bastard.

CADUCEUS, Mercury's wand.

CALIVER, light kind of musket.

CALLET, woman of ill repute.

CALLOT, coif worn on the wigs of our judges or serjeants-at-law (Gifford).

CALVERED, crimped, or sliced and pickled. (See Nares).

CAMOUCCIO, wretch, knave.

CAMUSED, flat.

CAN, knows.

CANDLE-RENT, rent from house property.

CANDLE-WASTER, one who studies late.

CANTER, sturdy beggar.

CAP OF MAINTENCE, an insignia of dignity, a cap of state borne before kings at their coronation; also an heraldic term.

CAPABLE, able to comprehend, fit to receive instruction, impression.

CAPANEUS, one of the "Seven against Thebes."

CARACT, carat, unit of weight for precious stones, etc.; value, worth.

CARANZA, Spanish author of a book on duelling.

CARCANET, jewelled ornament for the neck.

CARE, take care; object.

CAROSH, coach, carriage.

CARPET, table-cover.

CARRIAGE, bearing, behaviour.

CARWHITCHET, quip, pun.

CASAMATE, casemate, fortress.

CASE, a pair.

CASE, "in--," in condition.

CASSOCK, soldier's loose overcoat.

CAST, flight of hawks, couple.

CAST, throw dice; vomit; forecast, calculate.

CAST, cashiered.

CASTING-GLASS, bottle for sprinkling perfume.

CASTRIL, kestrel, falcon.

CAT, structure used in sieges.

CATAMITE, old form of "ganymede."

CATASTROPHE, conclusion.

CATCHPOLE, sheriff's officer.

CATES, dainties, provisions.

CATSO, rogue, cheat.

CAUTELOUS, crafty, artful.

CENSURE, criticism; sentence.

CENSURE, criticise; pass sentence, doom.

CERUSE, cosmetic containing white lead.

CESS, assess.

CHANGE, "hunt--," follow a fresh scent.

CHAPMAN, retail dealer.

CHARACTER, handwriting.

CHARGE, expense.

CHARM, subdue with magic, lay a spell on, silence.

CHARMING, exercising magic power.

CHARTEL, challenge.

CHEAP, bargain, market.

CHEAR, CHEER, comfort, encouragement; food, entertainment.

CHECK AT, aim reproof at.

CHEQUIN, gold Italian coin.

CHEVRIL, from kidskin, which is elastic and pliable.

CHIAUS, Turkish envoy; used for a cheat, swindler.

CHILDERMASS DAY, Innocents' Day.

CHOKE-BAIL, action which does not allow of bail.

CHRYSOPOEIA, alchemy.

CHRYSOSPERM, ways of producing gold.

CIBATION, adding fresh substances to supply the waste of evaporation.

CIMICI, bugs.

CINOPER, cinnabar.

CIOPPINI, chopine, lady's high shoe.

CIRCLING BOY, "a species of roarer; one who in some way drew a man into a snare, to cheat or rob him" (Nares).

CIRCUMSTANCE, circumlocution, beating about the bush; ceremony, everything pertaining to a certain condition; detail, particular.

CITRONISE, turn citron colour.

CITTERN, kind of guitar.

CITY-WIRES, woman of fashion, who made use of wires

for hair and dress.

CIVIL, legal.

CLAP, clack, chatter.

CLAPPER-DUDGEON, downright beggar.

CLAPS HIS DISH, a clap, or clack, dish (dish with a movable lid) was carried by beggars and lepers to show that the vessel was empty, and to give sound of their approach.

CLARIDIANA, heroine of an old romance.

CLARISSIMO, Venetian noble.

CLEM, starve.

CLICKET, latch.

CLIM O' THE CLOUGHS, etc., wordy heroes of romance.

CLIMATE, country.

CLOSE, secret, private; secretive.

CLOSENESS, secrecy.

CLOTH, arras, hangings.

CLOUT, mark shot at, bull's eye.

CLOWN, countryman, clodhopper.

COACH-LEAVES, folding blinds.

COALS, "bear no--," submit to no affront.

COAT-ARMOUR, coat of arms.

COAT-CARD, court-card.

COB-HERRING, HERRING-COB, a young herring.

COB-SWAN, male swan.

COCK-A-HOOP, denoting unstinted jollity; thought to be derived from turning on the tap that all might drink to the full of the flowing liquor.

COCKATRICE, reptile supposed to be produced from a cock's egg and to kill by its eye--used as a term of reproach for a woman.

COCK-BRAINED, giddy, wild.

COCKER, pamper.

COCKSCOMB, fool's cap.

COCKSTONE, stone said to be found in a cock's gizzard, and to possess particular virtues.

CODLING, softening by boiling.

COFFIN, raised crust of a pie.

COG, cheat, wheedle.

COIL, turmoil, confusion, ado.

COKELY, master of a puppet-show (Whalley).

COKES, fool, gull.

COLD-CONCEITED, having cold opinion of, coldly affected towards.

COLE-HARBOUR, a retreat for people of all sorts.

COLLECTION, composure; deduction.

COLLOP, small slice, piece of flesh.

COLLY, blacken.

COLOUR, pretext.

COLOURS, "fear no--," no enemy (quibble).

COLSTAFF, cowlstaff, pole for carrying a cowl=tub.

COME ABOUT, charge, turn round.

COMFORTABLE BREAD, spiced gingerbread.

COMING, forward, ready to respond, complaisant.

COMMENT, commentary; "sometime it is taken for a lie or fayned tale" (Bullokar, 1616).

COMMODITY, "current for--," allusion to practice of money-lenders, who forced the borrower to take part of the loan in the shape of worthless goods on which the latter had to make money if he could.

COMMUNICATE, share.

COMPASS, "in--," within the range, sphere.

COMPLEMENT, completion, completement; anything required for the perfecting or carrying out of a person or affair; accomplishment.

COMPLEXION, natural disposition, constitution.

COMPLIMENT, See Complement.

COMPLIMENTARIES, masters of accomplishments.

COMPOSITION, constitution; agreement, contract.

COMPOSURE, composition.

COMPTER, COUNTER, debtors' prison.

CONCEALMENT, a certain amount of church property had been retained at the dissolution of the monasteries; Elizabeth sent commissioners to search it out, and the courtiers begged for it.

CONCEIT, idea, fancy, witty invention, conception, opinion.

CONCEIT, apprehend.

CONCEITED, fancifully, ingeniously devised or conceived; possessed of intelligence, witty, ingenious (hence well conceited, etc.); disposed to joke; of opinion, possessed of an idea.

CONCEIVE, understand.

CONCENT, harmony, agreement.

CONCLUDE, infer, prove.

CONCOCT, assimilate, digest.

CONDEN'T, probably conducted.

CONDUCT, escort, conductor.

CONEY-CATCH, cheat.

CONFECT, sweetmeat.

CONFER, compare.

CONGIES, bows.

CONNIVE, give a look, wink, of secret intelligence.

CONSORT, company, concert.

CONSTANCY, fidelity, ardour, persistence.

CONSTANT, confirmed, persistent, faithful.

CONSTANTLY, firmly, persistently.

CONTEND, strive.

CONTINENT, holding together.

CONTROL (the point), bear or beat down.

CONVENT, assembly, meeting.

CONVERT, turn (oneself).

CONVEY, transmit from one to another.

CONVINCE, evince, prove; overcome, overpower; convict.

COP, head, top; tuft on head of birds; "a cop" may have reference to one or other meaning; Gifford and others interpret as "conical, terminating in a point."

COPE-MAN, chapman.

COPESMATE, companion.

COPY (Lat. copia), abundance, copiousness.

CORN ("powder--"), grain.

COROLLARY, finishing part or touch.

CORSIVE, corrosive.

CORTINE, curtain, (arch.) wall between two towers, etc.

CORYAT, famous for his travels, published as "Coryat's Crudities."

COSSET, pet lamb, pet.

COSTARD, head.

COSTARD-MONGER, apple-seller, coster-monger.

COSTS, ribs.

COTE, hut.

COTHURNAL, from "cothurnus," a particular boot worn by actors in Greek tragedy.

COTQUEAN, hussy.

COUNSEL, secret.

COUNTENANCE, means necessary for support; credit, standing.

COUNTER. See Compter.

COUNTER, pieces of metal or ivory for calculating at play.

COUNTER, "hunt--," follow scent in reverse direction.

COUNTERFEIT, false coin.

COUNTERPANE, one part or counterpart of a deed or indenture.

COUNTERPOINT, opposite, contrary point.

COURT-DISH, a kind of drinking-cup (Halliwell); N.E.D. quotes from Bp. Goodman's "Court of James I.": "The king...caused his carver to cut him out a court-dish, that is, something of every dish, which he sent him as part of his reversion," but this does not sound like short allowance or small receptacle.

COURT-DOR, fool.

COURTEAU, curtal, small horse with docked tail.

COURTSHIP, courtliness.

COVETISE, avarice.

COWSHARD, cow dung.

COXCOMB, fool's cap, fool.

COY, shrink; disdain.

COYSTREL, low varlet.

COZEN, cheat.

CRACK, lively young rogue, wag.

CRACK, crack up, boast; come to grief.

CRAMBE, game of crambo, in which the players find rhymes for a given word.

CRANCH, craunch.

CRANION, spider-like; also fairy appellation for a fly (Gifford, who refers to lines in Drayton's "Nimphidia").

CRIMP, game at cards.

CRINCLE, draw back, turn aside.

CRISPED, with curled or waved hair.

CROP, gather, reap.

CROPSHIRE, a kind of herring. (See N.E.D.)

CROSS, any piece of money, many coins being stamped with a cross.

CROSS AND PILE, heads and tails.

CROSSLET, crucible.

CROWD, fiddle.

CRUDITIES, undigested matter.

CRUMP, curl up.

CRUSADO, Portuguese gold coin, marked with a cross.

CRY ("he that cried Italian"), "speak in a musical cadence," intone, or declaim (?); cry up.

CUCKING-STOOL, used for the ducking of scolds, etc.

CUCURBITE, a gourd-shaped vessel used for distillation.

CUERPO, "in--," in undress.

CULLICE, broth.

CULLION, base fellow, coward.

CULLISEN, badge worn on their arm by servants.

CULVERIN, kind of cannon.

CUNNING, skill.

CUNNING, skilful.

CUNNING-MAN, fortune-teller.

CURE, care for.

CURIOUS(LY), scrupulous, particular; elaborate, elegant(ly), dainty(ly) (hence "in curious").

CURST, shrewish, mischievous.

CURTAL, dog with docked tail, of inferior sort.

CUSTARD, "quaking--," "--politic," reference to a large custard which formed part of a city feast and afforded huge entertainment, for the fool jumped into it, and other like tricks were played. (See "All's Well, etc." ii. 5, 40.)

CUTWORK, embroidery, open-work.

CYPRES (CYPRUS) (quibble), cypress (or cyprus) being a transparent material, and when black used for mourning.

DAGGER ("--frumety"), name of tavern.

DARGISON, apparently some person known in ballad or tale.

DAUPHIN MY BOY, refrain of old comic song.

DAW, daunt.

DEAD LIFT, desperate emergency.

DEAR, applied to that which in any way touches us nearly.

DECLINE, turn off from; turn away, aside.

DEFALK, deduct, abate.

DEFEND, forbid.

DEGENEROUS, degenerate.

DEGREES, steps.

DELATE, accuse.

DEMI-CULVERIN, cannon carrying a ball of about ten pounds.

DENIER, the smallest possible coin, being the twelfth part of a sou.

DEPART, part with.

DEPENDANCE, ground of quarrel in duello language.

DESERT, reward.

DESIGNMENT, design.

DESPERATE, rash, reckless.

DETECT, allow to be detected, betray, inform against.

DETERMINE, terminate.

DETRACT, draw back, refuse.

DEVICE, masque, show; a thing moved by wires, etc., puppet.

DEVISE, exact in every particular.

DEVISED, invented.

DIAPASM, powdered aromatic herbs, made into balls

of perfumed paste. (See Pomander.)

DIBBLE, (?) moustache (N.E.D.); (?) dagger (Cunningham).

DIFFUSED, disordered, scattered, irregular.

DIGHT, dressed.

DILDO, refrain of popular songs; vague term of low meaning.

DIMBLE, dingle, ravine.

DIMENSUM, stated allowance.

DISBASE, debase.

DISCERN, distinguish, show a difference between.

DISCHARGE, settle for.

DISCIPLINE, reformation; ecclesiastical system.

DISCLAIM, renounce all part in.

DISCOURSE, process of reasoning, reasoning faculty.

DISCOURTSHIP, discourtesy.

DISCOVER, betray, reveal; display.

DISFAVOUR, disfigure.

DISPARAGEMENT, legal term applied to the unfitness

in any way of a marriage arranged for in the case of wards.

DISPENSE WITH, grant dispensation for.

DISPLAY, extend.

DIS'PLE, discipline, teach by the whip.

DISPOSED, inclined to merriment.

DISPOSURE, disposal.

DISPRISE, depreciate.

DISPUNCT, not punctilious.

DISQUISITION, search.

DISSOLVED, enervated by grief.

DISTANCE, (?) proper measure.

DISTASTE, offence, cause of offence.

DISTASTE, render distasteful.

DISTEMPERED, upset, out of humour.

DIVISION (mus.), variation, modulation.

DOG-BOLT, term of contempt.

DOLE, given in dole, charity.

DOLE OF FACES, distribution of grimaces.

DOOM, verdict, sentence.

DOP, dip, low bow.

DOR, beetle, buzzing insect, drone, idler.

DOR, (?) buzz; "give the--," make a fool of.

DOSSER, pannier, basket.

DOTES, endowments, qualities.

DOTTEREL, plover; gull, fool.

DOUBLE, behave deceitfully.

DOXY, wench, mistress.

DRACHM, Greek silver coin.

DRESS, groom, curry.

DRESSING, coiffure.

DRIFT, intention.

DRYFOOT, track by mere scent of foot.

DUCKING, punishment for minor offences.

DUILL, grieve.

DUMPS, melancholy, originally a mournful melody.

DURINDANA, Orlando's sword.

DWINDLE, shrink away, be overawed.

EAN, yean, bring forth young.

EASINESS, readiness.

EBOLITION, ebullition.

EDGE, sword.

EECH, eke.

EGREGIOUS, eminently excellent.

EKE, also, moreover.

E-LA, highest note in the scale.

EGGS ON THE SPIT, important business on hand.

ELF-LOCK, tangled hair, supposed to be the work of elves.

EMMET, ant.

ENGAGE, involve.

ENGHLE. See Ingle.

ENGHLE, cajole; fondle.

ENGIN(E), device, contrivance; agent; ingenuity, wit.

ENGINER, engineer, deviser, plotter.

ENGINOUS, crafty, full of devices; witty, ingenious.

ENGROSS, monopolise.

ENS, an existing thing, a substance.

ENSIGNS, tokens, wounds.

ENSURE, assure.

ENTERTAIN, take into service.

ENTREAT, plead.

ENTREATY, entertainment.

ENTRY, place where a deer has lately passed.

ENVOY, denouement, conclusion.

ENVY, spite, calumny, dislike, odium.

EPHEMERIDES, calendars.

EQUAL, just, impartial.

ERECTION, elevation in esteem.

ERINGO, candied root of the sea-holly, formerly used as a sweetmeat and aphrodisiac.

ERRANT, arrant.

ESSENTIATE, become assimilated.

ESTIMATION, esteem.

ESTRICH, ostrich.

ETHNIC, heathen.

EURIPUS, flux and reflux.

EVEN, just equable.

EVENT, fate, issue.

EVENT(ED), issue(d).

EVERT, overturn.

EXACUATE, sharpen.

EXAMPLESS, without example or parallel.

EXCALIBUR, King Arthur's sword.

EXEMPLIFY, make an example of.

EXEMPT, separate, exclude.

EXEQUIES, obsequies.

EXHALE, drag out.

EXHIBITION, allowance for keep, pocket-money.

EXORBITANT, exceeding limits of propriety or law, inordinate.

EXORNATION, ornament.

EXPECT, wait.

EXPIATE, terminate.

EXPLICATE, explain, unfold.

EXTEMPORAL, extempore, unpremeditated.

EXTRACTION, essence.

EXTRAORDINARY, employed for a special or temporary purpose.

EXTRUDE, expel.

EYE, "in--," in view.

EYEBRIGHT, (?) a malt liquor in which the herb of this name was infused, or a person who sold the same (Gifford).

EYE-TINGE, least shade or gleam.

FACE, appearance.

FACES ABOUT, military word of command.

FACINOROUS, extremely wicked.

FACKINGS, faith.

FACT, deed, act, crime.

FACTIOUS, seditious, belonging to a party, given to party feeling.

FAECES, dregs.

FAGIOLI, French beans.

FAIN, forced, necessitated.

FAITHFUL, believing.

FALL, ruff or band turned back on the shoulders; or, veil.

FALSIFY, feign (fencing term).

FAME, report.

FAMILIAR, attendant spirit.

FANTASTICAL, capricious, whimsical.

FARCE, stuff.

FAR-FET. See Fet.

FARTHINGAL, hooped petticoat.

FAUCET, tapster.

FAULT, lack; loss, break in line of scent; "for--," in default of.

FAUTOR, partisan.

FAYLES, old table game similar to backgammon.

FEAR(ED), affright(ed).

FEAT, activity, operation; deed, action.

FEAT, elegant, trim.

FEE, "in--" by feudal obligation.

FEIZE, beat, belabour.

FELLOW, term of contempt.

FENNEL, emblem of flattery.

FERE, companion, fellow.

FERN-SEED, supposed to have power of rendering invisible.

FET, fetched.

FETCH, trick.

FEUTERER (Fr. vautrier), dog-keeper.

FEWMETS, dung.

FICO, fig.

FIGGUM, (?) jugglery.

FIGMENT, fiction, invention.

FIRK, frisk, move suddenly, or in jerks; "--up," stir up, rouse; "firks mad," suddenly behaves like a madman.

FIT, pay one out, punish.

FITNESS, readiness.

FITTON (FITTEN), lie, invention.

FIVE-AND-FIFTY, "highest number to stand on at primero" (Gifford).

FLAG, to fly low and waveringly.

FLAGON CHAIN, for hanging a smelling-bottle (Fr. flacon) round the neck (?). (See N.E.D.).

FLAP-DRAGON, game similar to snap-dragon.

FLASKET, some kind of basket.

FLAW, sudden gust or squall of wind.

FLAWN, custard.

FLEA, catch fleas.

FLEER, sneer, laugh derisively.

FLESH, feed a hawk or dog with flesh to incite it to the chase; initiate in blood-shed; satiate.

FLICKER-MOUSE, bat.

FLIGHT, light arrow.

FLITTER-MOUSE, bat.

FLOUT, mock, speak and act contemptuously.

FLOWERS, pulverised substance.

FLY, familiar spirit.

FOIL, weapon used in fencing; that which sets anything off to advantage.

FOIST, cut-purse, sharper.

FOND(LY), foolish(ly).

FOOT-CLOTH, housings of ornamental cloth which

hung down on either side a horse to the ground.

FOOTING, foothold; footstep; dancing.

FOPPERY, foolery.

FOR, "--failing," for fear of failing.

FORBEAR, bear with; abstain from.

FORCE, "hunt at--," run the game down with dogs.

FOREHEAD, modesty; face, assurance, effrontery.

FORESLOW, delay.

FORESPEAK, bewitch; foretell.

FORETOP, front lock of hair which fashion required to be worn upright.

FORGED, fabricated.

FORM, state formally.

FORMAL, shapely; normal; conventional.

FORTHCOMING, produced when required.

FOUNDER, disable with over-riding.

FOURM, form, lair.

FOX, sword.

FRAIL, rush basket in which figs or raisins were packed.

FRAMPULL, peevish, sour-tempered.

FRAPLER, blusterer, wrangler.

FRAYING, "a stag is said to fray his head when he rubs it against a tree to...cause the outward coat of the new horns to fall off" (Gifford).

FREIGHT (of the gazetti), burden (of the newspapers).

FREQUENT, full.

FRICACE, rubbing.

FRICATRICE, woman of low character.

FRIPPERY, old clothes shop.

FROCK, smock-frock.

FROLICS, (?) humorous verses circulated at a feast (N.E.D.); couplets wrapped round sweetmeats (Cunningham).

FRONTLESS, shameless.

FROTED, rubbed.

FRUMETY, hulled wheat boiled in milk and spiced.

FRUMP, flout, sneer.

FUCUS, dye.

FUGEAND, (?) figent: fidgety, restless (N.E.D.).

FULLAM, false dice.

FULMART, polecat.

FULSOME, foul, offensive.

FURIBUND, raging, furious.

GALLEY-FOIST, city-barge, used on Lord Mayor's Day, when he was sworn into his office at Westminster (Whalley).

GALLIARD, lively dance in triple time.

GAPE, be eager after.

GARAGANTUA, Rabelais' giant.

GARB, sheaf (Fr. gerbe); manner, fashion, behaviour.

GARD, guard, trimming, gold or silver lace, or other ornament.

GARDED, faced or trimmed.

GARNISH, fee.

GAVEL-KIND, name of a land-tenure existing chiefly in Kent; from 16th century often used to denote custom of dividing a deceased man's property equally among his sons (N.E.D.).

GAZETTE, small Venetian coin worth about three-farthings.

GEANCE, jaunt, errand.

GEAR (GEER), stuff, matter, affair.

GELID, frozen.

GEMONIES, steps from which the bodies of criminals were thrown into the river.

GENERAL, free, affable.

GENIUS, attendant spirit.

GENTRY, gentlemen; manners characteristic of gentry, good breeding.

GIB-CAT, tom-cat.

GIGANTOMACHIZE, start a giants' war.

GIGLOT, wanton.

GIMBLET, gimlet.

GING, gang.

GLASS ("taking in of shadows, etc."), crystal or beryl.

GLEEK, card game played by three; party of three, trio; side glance.

GLICK (GLEEK), jest, gibe.

GLIDDER, glaze.

GLORIOUSLY, of vain glory.

GODWIT, bird of the snipe family.

GOLD-END-MAN, a buyer of broken gold and silver.

GOLL, hand.

GONFALIONIER, standard-bearer, chief magistrate, etc.

GOOD, sound in credit.

GOOD-YEAR, good luck.

GOOSE-TURD, colour of. (See Turd).

GORCROW, carrion crow.

GORGET, neck armour.

GOSSIP, godfather.

GOWKED, from "gowk," to stand staring and gaping like

a fool.

GRANNAM, grandam.

GRASS, (?) grease, fat.

GRATEFUL, agreeable, welcome.

GRATIFY, give thanks to.

GRATITUDE, gratuity.

GRATULATE, welcome, congratulate.

GRAVITY, dignity.

GRAY, badger.

GRICE, cub.

GRIEF, grievance.

GRIPE, vulture, griffin.

GRIPE'S EGG, vessel in shape of.

GROAT, fourpence.

GROGRAN, coarse stuff made of silk and mohair, or of coarse silk.

GROOM-PORTER, officer in the royal household.

GROPE, handle, probe.

GROUND, pit (hence "grounded judgments").

GUARD, caution, heed.

GUARDANT, heraldic term: turning the head only.

GUILDER, Dutch coin worth about 4d.

GULES, gullet, throat; heraldic term for red.

GULL, simpleton, dupe.

GUST, taste.

HAB NAB, by, on, chance.

HABERGEON, coat of mail.

HAGGARD, wild female hawk; hence coy, wild.

HALBERD, combination of lance and battle-axe.

HALL, "a--!" a cry to clear the room for the dancers.

HANDSEL, first money taken.

HANGER, loop or strap on a sword-belt from which the sword was suspended.

HAP, fortune, luck.

HAPPILY, haply.

HAPPINESS, appropriateness, fitness.

HAPPY, rich.

HARBOUR, track, trace (an animal) to its shelter.

HARD-FAVOURED, harsh-featured.

HARPOCRATES, Horus the child, son of Osiris, figured with a finger pointing to his mouth, indicative of silence.

HARRINGTON, a patent was granted to Lord H. for the coinage of tokens (q.v.).

HARROT, herald.

HARRY NICHOLAS, founder of a community called the "Family of Love."

HAY, net for catching rabbits, etc.

HAY! (Ital. hai!), you have it (a fencing term).

HAY IN HIS HORN, ill-tempered person.

HAZARD, game at dice; that which is staked.

HEAD, "first--," young deer with antlers first sprouting; fig. a newly-ennobled man.

HEADBOROUGH, constable.

HEARKEN AFTER, inquire; "hearken out," find, search out.

HEARTEN, encourage.

HEAVEN AND HELL ("Alchemist"), names of taverns.

HECTIC, fever.

HEDGE IN, include.

HELM, upper part of a retort.

HER'NSEW, hernshaw, heron.

HIERONIMO (JERONIMO), hero of Kyd's "Spanish Tragedy."

HOBBY, nag.

HOBBY-HORSE, imitation horse of some light material, fastened round the waist of the morrice-dancer, who imitated the movements of a skittish horse.

HODDY-DODDY, fool.

HOIDEN, hoyden, formerly applied to both sexes (ancient term for leveret? Gifford).

HOLLAND, name of two famous chemists.

HONE AND HONERO, wailing expressions of lament or discontent.

HOOD-WINK'D, blindfolded.

HORARY, hourly.

HORN-MAD, stark mad (quibble).

HORN-THUMB, cut-purses were in the habit of wearing a horn shield on the thumb.

HORSE-BREAD-EATING, horses were often fed on coarse bread.

HORSE-COURSER, horse-dealer.

HOSPITAL, Christ's Hospital.

HOWLEGLAS, Eulenspiegel, the hero of a popular German tale which relates his buffooneries and knavish tricks.

HUFF, hectoring, arrogance.

HUFF IT, swagger.

HUISHER (Fr. huissier), usher.

HUM, beer and spirits mixed together.

HUMANITIAN, humanist, scholar.

HUMOROUS, capricious, moody, out of humour; moist.

HUMOUR, a word used in and out of season in the time of Shakespeare and Ben Jonson, and ridiculed by both.

HUMOURS, manners.

HUMPHREY, DUKE, those who were dinnerless spent the dinner-hour in a part of St. Paul's where stood a monument said to be that of the duke's; hence "dine with Duke Humphrey," to go hungry.

HURTLESS, harmless.

IDLE, useless, unprofitable.

ILL-AFFECTED, ill-disposed.

ILL-HABITED, unhealthy.

ILLUSTRATE, illuminate.

IMBIBITION, saturation, steeping.

IMBROCATA, fencing term: a thrust in tierce.

IMPAIR, impairment.

IMPART, give money.

IMPARTER, any one ready to be cheated and to part with his money.

IMPEACH, damage.

IMPERTINENCIES, irrelevancies.

IMPERTINENT(LY), irrelevant(ly), without reason or purpose.

IMPOSITION, duty imposed by.

IMPOTENTLY, beyond power of control.

IMPRESS, money in advance.

IMPULSION, incitement.

IN AND IN, a game played by two or three persons with four dice.

INCENSE, incite, stir up.

INCERATION, act of covering with wax; or reducing a substance to softness of wax.

INCH, "to their--es," according to their stature, capabilities.

INCH-PIN, sweet-bread.

INCONVENIENCE, inconsistency, absurdity.

INCONY, delicate, rare (used as a term of affection).

INCUBEE, incubus.

INCUBUS, evil spirit that oppresses us in sleep, nightmare.

INCURIOUS, unfastidious, uncritical.

INDENT, enter into engagement.

INDIFFERENT, tolerable, passable.

INDIGESTED, shapeless, chaotic.

INDUCE, introduce.

INDUE, supply.

INEXORABLE, relentless.

INFANTED, born, produced.

INFLAME, augment charge.

INGENIOUS, used indiscriminantly for ingenuous; intelligent, talented.

INGENUITY, ingenuousness.

INGENUOUS, generous.

INGINE. See Engin.

INGINER, engineer. (See Enginer).

INGLE, OR ENGHLE, bosom friend, intimate, minion.

INHABITABLE, uninhabitable.

INJURY, insult, affront.

IN-MATE, resident, indwelling.

INNATE, natural.

INNOCENT, simpleton.

INQUEST, jury, or other official body of inquiry.

INQUISITION, inquiry.

INSTANT, immediate.

INSTRUMENT, legal document.

INSURE, assure.

INTEGRATE, complete, perfect.

INTELLIGENCE, secret information, news.

INTEND, note carefully, attend, give ear to, be occupied with.

INTENDMENT, intention.

INTENT, intention, wish.

INTENTION, concentration of attention or gaze.

INTENTIVE, attentive.

INTERESSED, implicated.

INTRUDE, bring in forcibly or without leave.

INVINCIBLY, invisibly.

INWARD, intimate.

IRPE (uncertain), "a fantastic grimace, or contortion of the body: (Gifford)."

JACK, Jack o' the clock, automaton figure that strikes the hour; Jack-a-lent, puppet thrown at in Lent.

JACK, key of a virginal.

JACOB'S STAFF, an instrument for taking altitudes and distances.

JADE, befool.

JEALOUSY, JEALOUS, suspicion, suspicious.

JERKING, lashing.

JEW'S TRUMP, Jew's harp.

JIG, merry ballad or tune; a fanciful dialogue or light comic act introduced at the end or during an interlude of a play.

JOINED (JOINT)-STOOL, folding stool.

JOLL, jowl.

JOLTHEAD, blockhead.

JUMP, agree, tally.

JUST YEAR, no one was capable of the consulship until he was forty-three.

KELL, cocoon.

KELLY, an alchemist.

KEMB, comb.

KEMIA, vessel for distillation.

KIBE, chap, sore.

KILDERKIN, small barrel.

KILL, kiln.

KIND, nature; species; "do one's--," act according to one's nature.

KIRTLE, woman's gown of jacket and petticoat.

KISS OR DRINK AFORE ME, "this is a familiar expression, employed when what the speaker is just about to say is anticipated by another" (Gifford).

KIT, fiddle.

KNACK, snap, click.

KNIPPER-DOLING, a well-known Anabaptist.

KNITTING CUP, marriage cup.

KNOCKING, striking, weighty.

KNOT, company, band; a sandpiper or robin snipe (Tringa canutus); flower-bed laid out in fanciful design.

KURSINED, KYRSIN, christened.

LABOURED, wrought with labour and care.

LADE, load(ed).

LADING, load.

LAID, plotted.

LANCE-KNIGHT (Lanzknecht), a German mercenary foot-soldier.

LAP, fold.

LAR, household god.

LARD, garnish.

LARGE, abundant.

LARUM, alarum, call to arms.

LATTICE, tavern windows were furnished with lattices of various colours.

LAUNDER, to wash gold in aqua regia, so as imperceptibly to extract some of it.

LAVE, ladle, bale.

LAW, "give--," give a start (term of chase).

LAXATIVE, loose.

LAY ABOARD, run alongside generally with intent to board.

LEAGUER, siege, or camp of besieging army.

LEASING, lying.

LEAVE, leave off, desist.

LEER, leering or "empty, hence, perhaps, leer horse, a horse without a rider; leer is an adjective meaning uncontrolled, hence 'leer drunkards'" (Halliwell); according to Nares, a leer (empty) horse meant also a led horse; leeward, left.

LEESE, lose.

LEGS, "make--," do obeisance.

LEIGER, resident representative.

LEIGERITY, legerdemain.

LEMMA, subject proposed, or title of the epigram.

LENTER, slower.

LET, hinder.

LET, hindrance.

LEVEL COIL, a rough game...in which one hunted another from his seat. Hence used for any noisy riot (Halliwell).

LEWD, ignorant.

LEYSTALLS, receptacles of filth.

LIBERAL, ample.

LIEGER, ledger, register.

LIFT(ING), steal(ing); theft.

LIGHT, alight.

LIGHTLY, commonly, usually, often.

LIKE, please.

LIKELY, agreeable, pleasing.

LIME-HOUND, leash-, blood-hound.

LIMMER, vile, worthless.

LIN, leave off.

Line, "by--," by rule.

LINSTOCK, staff to stick in the ground, with forked head to hold a lighted match for firing cannon.

LIQUID, clear.

LIST, listen, hark; like, please.

LIVERY, legal term, delivery of the possession, etc.

LOGGET, small log, stick.

LOOSE, solution; upshot, issue; release of an arrow.

LOSE, give over, desist from; waste.

LOUTING, bowing, cringing.

LUCULENT, bright of beauty.

LUDGATHIANS, dealers on Ludgate Hill.

LURCH, rob, cheat.

LUTE, to close a vessel with some kind of cement.

MACK, unmeaning expletive.

MADGE-HOWLET or OWL, barn-owl.

MAIM, hurt, injury.

MAIN, chief concern (used as a quibble on heraldic term for "hand").

MAINPRISE, becoming surety for a prisoner so as to procure his release.

MAINTENANCE, giving aid, or abetting.

MAKE, mate.

MAKE, MADE, acquaint with business, prepare(d), instruct(ed).

MALLANDERS, disease of horses.

MALT HORSE, dray horse.

MAMMET, puppet.

MAMMOTHREPT, spoiled child.

MANAGE, control (term used for breaking-in horses); handling, administration.

MANGO, slave-dealer.

MANGONISE, polish up for sale.

MANIPLES, bundles, handfuls.

MANKIND, masculine, like a virago.

MANKIND, humanity.

MAPLE FACE, spotted face (N.E.D.).

MARCHPANE, a confection of almonds, sugar, etc.

MARK, "fly to the--," "generally said of a goshawk when, having 'put in' a covey of partridges, she takes stand, marking the spot where they disappeared from view until the falconer arrives to put them out to her" (Harting, Bibl. Accip. Gloss. 226).

MARLE, marvel.

MARROW-BONE MAN, one often on his knees for prayer.

MARRY! exclamation derived from the Virgin's name.

MARRY GIP, "probably originated from By Mary Gipcy" = St. Mary of Egypt, (N.E.D.).

MARTAGAN, Turk's cap lily.

MARYHINCHCO, stringhalt.

MASORETH, Masora, correct form of the scriptural text according to Hebrew tradition.

MASS, abb. for master.

MAUND, beg.

MAUTHER, girl, maid.

MEAN, moderation.

MEASURE, dance, more especially a stately one.

MEAT, "carry--in one's mouth," be a source of money or entertainment.

MEATH, metheglin.

MECHANICAL, belonging to mechanics, mean, vulgar.

MEDITERRANEO, middle aisle of St. Paul's, a general resort for business and amusement.

MEET WITH, even with.

MELICOTTON, a late kind of peach.

MENSTRUE, solvent.

MERCAT, market.

MERD, excrement.

MERE, undiluted; absolute, unmitigated.

MESS, party of four.

METHEGLIN, fermented liquor, of which one ingredient was honey.

METOPOSCOPY, study of physiognomy.

MIDDLING GOSSIP, go-between.

MIGNIARD, dainty, delicate.

MILE-END, training-ground of the city.

MINE-MEN, sappers.

MINION, form of cannon.

MINSITIVE, (?) mincing, affected (N.E.D.).

MISCELLANY MADAM, "a female trader in miscellaneous articles; a dealer in trinkets or ornaments of various kinds, such as kept shops in the New Exchange" (Nares).

MISCELLINE, mixed grain; medley.

MISCONCEIT, misconception.

MISPRISE, MISPRISION, mistake, misunderstanding.

MISTAKE AWAY, carry away as if by mistake.

MITHRIDATE, an antidote against poison.

MOCCINIGO, small Venetian coin, worth about ninepence.

MODERN, in the mode; ordinary, commonplace.

MOMENT, force or influence of value.

MONTANTO, upward stroke.

MONTH'S MIND, violent desire.

MOORISH, like a moor or waste.

MORGLAY, sword of Bevis of Southampton.

MORRICE-DANCE, dance on May Day, etc., in which certain personages were represented.

MORTALITY, death.

MORT-MAL, old sore, gangrene.

MOSCADINO, confection flavoured with musk.

MOTHER, Hysterica passio.

MOTION, proposal, request; puppet, puppet-show; "one of the small figures on the face of a large clock which was moved by the vibration of the pendulum" (Whalley).

MOTION, suggest, propose.

MOTLEY, parti-coloured dress of a fool; hence used to signify pertaining to, or like, a fool.

MOTTE, motto.

MOURNIVAL, set of four aces or court cards in a hand; a quartette.

MOW, setord hay or sheaves of grain.

MUCH! expressive of irony and incredulity.

MUCKINDER, handkerchief.

MULE, "born to ride on--," judges or serjeants-at-law formerly rode on mules when going in state to Westminster (Whally).

MULLETS, small pincers.

MUM-CHANCE, game of chance, played in silence.

MUN, must.

MUREY, dark crimson red.

MUSCOVY-GLASS, mica.

MUSE, wonder.

MUSICAL, in harmony.

MUSS, mouse; scramble.

MYROBOLANE, foreign conserve, "a dried plum, brought from the Indies."

MYSTERY, art, trade, profession.

NAIL, "to the--" (ad unguem), to perfection, to the

very utmost.

NATIVE, natural.

NEAT, cattle.

NEAT, smartly apparelled; unmixed; dainty.

NEATLY, neatly finished.

NEATNESS, elegance.

NEIS, nose, scent.

NEUF (NEAF, NEIF), fist.

NEUFT, newt.

NIAISE, foolish, inexperienced person.

NICE, fastidious, trivial, finical, scrupulous.

NICENESS, fastidiousness.

NICK, exact amount; right moment; "set in the--," meaning uncertain.

NICE, suit, fit; hit, seize the right moment, etc., exactly hit on, hit off.

NOBLE, gold coin worth 6s. 8d.

NOCENT, harmful.

NIL, not will.

NOISE, company of musicians.

NOMENTACK, an Indian chief from Virginia.

NONES, nonce.

NOTABLE, egregious.

NOTE, sign, token.

NOUGHT, "be--," go to the devil, be hanged, etc.

NOWT-HEAD, blockhead.

NUMBER, rhythm.

NUPSON, oaf, simpleton.

OADE, woad.

OBARNI, preparation of mead.

OBJECT, oppose; expose; interpose.

OBLATRANT, barking, railing.

OBNOXIOUS, liable, exposed; offensive.

OBSERVANCE, homage, devoted service.

OBSERVANT, attentive, obsequious.

OBSERVE, show deference, respect.

OBSERVER, one who shows deference, or waits upon another.

OBSTANCY, legal phrase, "juridical opposition."

OBSTREPEROUS, clamorous, vociferous.

OBSTUPEFACT, stupefied.

ODLING, (?) "must have some relation to tricking and cheating" (Nares).

OMINOUS, deadly, fatal.

ONCE, at once; for good and all; used also for additional emphasis.

ONLY, pre-eminent, special.

OPEN, make public; expound.

OPPILATION, obstruction.

OPPONE, oppose.

OPPOSITE, antagonist.

OPPRESS, suppress.

ORIGINOUS, native.

ORT, remnant, scrap.

OUT, "to be--," to have forgotten one's part; not at one with each other.

OUTCRY, sale by auction.

OUTRECUIDANCE, arrogance, presumption.

OUTSPEAK, speak more than.

OVERPARTED, given too difficult a part to play.

OWLSPIEGEL. See Howleglass.

OYEZ! (O YES!), hear ye! call of the public crier when about to make a proclamation.

PACKING PENNY, "give a--," dismiss, send packing.

PAD, highway.

PAD-HORSE, road-horse.

PAINED (PANED) SLOPS, full breeches made of strips of different colour and material.

PAINFUL, diligent, painstaking.

PAINT, blush.

PALINODE, ode of recantation.

PALL, weaken, dim, make stale.

PALM, triumph.

PAN, skirt of dress or coat.

PANNEL, pad, or rough kind of saddle.

PANNIER-ALLY, inhabited by tripe-sellers.

PANNIER-MAN, hawker; a man employed about the inns of court to bring in provisions, set the table, etc.

PANTOFLE, indoor shoe, slipper.

PARAMENTOS, fine trappings.

PARANOMASIE, a play upon words.

PARANTORY, (?) peremptory.

PARCEL, particle, fragment (used contemptuously); article.

PARCEL, part, partly.

PARCEL-POET, poetaster.

PARERGA, subordinate matters.

PARGET, to paint or plaster the face.

PARLE, parley.

PARLOUS, clever, shrewd.

PART, apportion.

PARTAKE, participate in.

PARTED, endowed, talented.

PARTICULAR, individual person.

PARTIZAN, kind of halberd.

PARTRICH, partridge.

PARTS, qualities, endowments.

PASH, dash, smash.

PASS, care, trouble oneself.

PASSADO, fencing term: a thrust.

PASSAGE, game at dice.

PASSINGLY, exceedingly.

PASSION, effect caused by external agency.

PASSION, "in--," in so melancholy a tone, so pathetically.

PATOUN, (?) Fr. Paton, pellet of dough; perhaps the "moulding of the tobacco...for the pipe" (Gifford); (?)

variant of Petun, South American name of tobacco.

PATRICO, the recorder, priest, orator of strolling beggars or gipsies.

PATTEN, shoe with wooden sole; "go--," keep step with, accompany.

PAUCA VERBA, few words.

PAVIN, a stately dance.

PEACE, "with my master's--," by leave, favour.

PECULIAR, individual, single.

PEDANT, teacher of the languages.

PEEL, baker's shovel.

PEEP, speak in a small or shrill voice.

PEEVISH(LY), foolish(ly), capricious(ly); childish(ly).

PELICAN, a retort fitted with tube or tubes, for continuous distillation.

PENCIL, small tuft of hair.

PERDUE, soldier accustomed to hazardous service.

PEREMPTORY, resolute, bold; imperious; thorough, utter, absolute(ly).

PERIMETER, circumference of a figure.

PERIOD, limit, end.

PERK, perk up.

PERPETUANA, "this seems to be that glossy kind of stuff now called everlasting, and anciently worn by serjeants and other city officers" (Gifford).

PERSPECTIVE, a view, scene or scenery; an optical device which gave a distortion to the picture unless seen from a particular point; a relief, modelled to produce an optical illusion.

PERSPICIL, optic glass.

PERSTRINGE, criticise, censure.

PERSUADE, inculcate, commend.

PERSWAY, mitigate.

PERTINACY, pertinacity.

PESTLING, pounding, pulverising, like a pestle.

PETASUS, broad-brimmed hat or winged cap worn by Mercury.

PETITIONARY, supplicatory.

PETRONEL, a kind of carbine or light gun carried by horsemen.

PETULANT, pert, insolent.

PHERE. See Fere.

PHLEGMA, watery distilled liquor (old chem. "water").

PHRENETIC, madman.

PICARDIL, stiff upright collar fastened on to the coat (Whalley).

PICT-HATCH, disreputable quarter of London.

PIECE, person, used for woman or girl; a gold coin worth in Jonson's time 20s. or 22s.

PIECES OF EIGHT, Spanish coin: piastre equal to eight reals.

PIED, variegated.

PIE-POUDRES (Fr. pied-poudreux, dusty-foot), court held at fairs to administer justice to itinerant vendors and buyers.

PILCHER, term of contempt; one who wore a buff or leather jerkin, as did the serjeants of the counter; a pilferer.

PILED, pilled, peeled, bald.

PILL'D, polled, fleeced.

PIMLICO, "sometimes spoken of as a person--perhaps master of a house famous for a particular ale" (Gifford).

PINE, afflict, distress.

PINK, stab with a weapon; pierce or cut in scallops for ornament.

PINNACE, a go-between in infamous sense.

PISMIRE, ant.

PISTOLET, gold coin, worth about 6s.

PITCH, height of a bird of prey's flight.

PLAGUE, punishment, torment.

PLAIN, lament.

PLAIN SONG, simple melody.

PLAISE, plaice.

PLANET, "struck with a--," planets were supposed to have powers of blasting or exercising secret influences.

PLAUSIBLE, pleasing.

PLAUSIBLY, approvingly.

PLOT, plan.

PLY, apply oneself to.

POESIE, posy, motto inside a ring.

POINT IN HIS DEVICE, exact in every particular.

POINTS, tagged laces or cords for fastening the breeches to the doublet.

POINT-TRUSSER, one who trussed (tied) his master's points (q.v.).

POISE, weigh, balance.

POKING-STICK, stick used for setting the plaits of ruffs.

POLITIC, politician.

POLITIC, judicious, prudent, political.

POLITICIAN, plotter, intriguer.

POLL, strip, plunder, gain by extortion.

POMANDER, ball of perfume, worn or hung about the person to prevent infection, or for foppery.

POMMADO, vaulting on a horse without the aid of stirrups.

PONTIC, sour.

POPULAR, vulgar, of the populace.

POPULOUS, numerous.

PORT, gate; print of a deer's foot.

PORT, transport.

PORTAGUE, Portuguese gold coin, worth over 3 or 4 pounds.

PORTCULLIS, "--of coin," some old coins have a portcullis stamped on their reverse (Whalley).

PORTENT, marvel, prodigy; sinister omen.

PORTENTOUS, prophesying evil, threatening.

PORTER, references appear "to allude to Parsons, the king's porter, who was...near seven feet high" (Whalley).

POSSESS, inform, acquaint.

POST AND PAIR, a game at cards.

POSY, motto. (See Poesie).

POTCH, poach.

POULT-FOOT, club-foot.

POUNCE, claw, talon.

PRACTICE, intrigue, concerted plot.

PRACTISE, plot, conspire.

PRAGMATIC, an expert, agent.

PRAGMATIC, officious, conceited, meddling.

PRECEDENT, record of proceedings.

PRECEPT, warrant, summons.

PRECISIAN(ISM), Puritan(ism), preciseness.

PREFER, recommend.

PRESENCE, presence chamber.

PRESENT(LY), immediate(ly), without delay; at the present time; actually.

PRESS, force into service.

PREST, ready.

PRETEND, assert, allege.

PREVENT, anticipate.

PRICE, worth, excellence.

PRICK, point, dot used in the writing of Hebrew and other languages.

PRICK, prick out, mark off, select; trace, track;

"--away," make off with speed.

PRIMERO, game of cards.

PRINCOX, pert boy.

PRINT, "in--," to the letter, exactly.

PRISTINATE, former.

PRIVATE, private interests.

PRIVATE, privy, intimate.

PROCLIVE, prone to.

PRODIGIOUS, monstrous, unnatural.

PRODIGY, monster.

PRODUCED, prolonged.

PROFESS, pretend.

PROJECTION, the throwing of the "powder of projection" into the crucible to turn the melted metal into gold or silver.

PROLATE, pronounce drawlingly.

PROPER, of good appearance, handsome; own, particular.

PROPERTIES, stage necessaries.

PROPERTY, duty; tool.

PRORUMPED, burst out.

PROTEST, vow, proclaim (an affected word of that time); formally declare non-payment, etc., of bill of exchange; fig. failure of personal credit, etc.

PROVANT, soldier's allowance--hence, of common make.

PROVIDE, foresee.

PROVIDENCE, foresight, prudence.

PUBLICATION, making a thing public of common property (N.E.D.).

PUCKFIST, puff-ball; insipid, insignificant, boasting fellow.

PUFF-WING, shoulder puff.

PUISNE, judge of inferior rank, a junior.

PULCHRITUDE, beauty.

PUMP, shoe.

PUNGENT, piercing.

PUNTO, point, hit.

PURCEPT, precept, warrant.

PURE, fine, capital, excellent.

PURELY, perfectly, utterly.

PURL, pleat or fold of a ruff.

PURSE-NET, net of which the mouth is drawn together with a string.

PURSUIVANT, state messenger who summoned the persecuted seminaries; warrant officer.

PURSY, PURSINESS, shortwinded(ness).

PUT, make a push, exert yourself (N.E.D.).

PUT OFF, excuse, shift.

PUT ON, incite, encourage; proceed with, take in hand, try.

QUACKSALVER, quack.

QUAINT, elegant, elaborated, ingenious, clever.

QUAR, quarry.

QUARRIED, seized, or fed upon, as prey.

QUEAN, hussy, jade.

QUEASY, hazardous, delicate.

QUELL, kill, destroy.

QUEST, request; inquiry.

QUESTION, decision by force of arms.

QUESTMAN, one appointed to make official inquiry.

QUIB, QUIBLIN, quibble, quip.

QUICK, the living.

QUIDDIT, quiddity, legal subtlety.

QUIRK, clever turn or trick.

QUIT, requite, repay; acquit, absolve; rid; forsake, leave.

QUITTER-BONE, disease of horses.

QUODLING, codling.

QUOIT, throw like a quoit, chuck.

QUOTE, take note, observe, write down.

RACK, neck of mutton or pork (Halliwell).

RAKE UP, cover over.

RAMP, rear, as a lion, etc.

RAPT, carry away.

RAPT, enraptured.

RASCAL, young or inferior deer.

RASH, strike with a glancing oblique blow, as a boar with its tusk.

RATSEY, GOMALIEL, a famous highwayman.

RAVEN, devour.

REACH, understand.

REAL, regal.

REBATU, ruff, turned-down collar.

RECTOR, RECTRESS, director, governor.

REDARGUE, confute.

REDUCE, bring back.

REED, rede, counsel, advice.

REEL, run riot.

REFEL, refute.

REFORMADOES, disgraced or disbanded soldiers.

REGIMENT, government.

REGRESSION, return.

REGULAR ("Tale of a Tub"), regular noun (quibble) (N.E.D.).

RELIGION, "make--of," make a point of, scruple of.

RELISH, savour.

REMNANT, scrap of quotation.

REMORA, species of fish.

RENDER, depict, exhibit, show.

REPAIR, reinstate.

REPETITION, recital, narration.

REREMOUSE, bat.

RESIANT, resident.

RESIDENCE, sediment.

RESOLUTION, judgment, decision.

RESOLVE, inform; assure; prepare, make up one's mind; dissolve; come to a decision, be convinced; relax, set at ease.

RESPECTIVE, worthy of respect; regardful, discriminative.

RESPECTIVELY, with reverence.

RESPECTLESS, regardless.

RESPIRE, exhale; inhale.

RESPONSIBLE, correspondent.

REST, musket-rest.

REST, "set up one's--," venture one's all, one's last stake (from game of primero).

REST, arrest.

RESTIVE, RESTY, dull, inactive.

RETCHLESS(NESS), reckless(ness).

RETIRE, cause to retire.

RETRICATO, fencing term.

RETRIEVE, rediscovery of game once sprung.

RETURNS, ventures sent abroad, for the safe return of which so much money is received.

REVERBERATE, dissolve or blend by reflected heat.

REVERSE, REVERSO, back-handed thrust, etc., in fencing.

REVISE, reconsider a sentence.

RHEUM, spleen, caprice.

RIBIBE, abusive term for an old woman.

RID, destroy, do away with.

RIFLING, raffling, dicing.

RING, "cracked within the--," coins so cracked were unfit for currency.

RISSE, risen, rose.

RIVELLED, wrinkled.

ROARER, swaggerer.

ROCHET, fish of the gurnet kind.

ROCK, distaff.

RODOMONTADO, braggadocio.

ROGUE, vagrant, vagabond.

RONDEL, "a round mark in the score of a public-house" (Nares); roundel.

ROOK, sharper; fool, dupe.

ROSAKER, similar to ratsbane.

ROSA-SOLIS, a spiced spirituous liquor.

ROSES, rosettes.

ROUND, "gentlemen of the--," officers of inferior rank.

ROUND TRUNKS, trunk hose, short loose breeches reaching almost or quite to the knees.

ROUSE, carouse, bumper.

ROVER, arrow used for shooting at a random mark at uncertain distance.

ROWLY-POWLY, roly-poly.

RUDE, RUDENESS, unpolished, rough(ness), coarse(ness).

RUFFLE, flaunt, swagger.

RUG, coarse frieze.

RUG-GOWNS, gown made of rug.

RUSH, reference to rushes with which the floors were then strewn.

RUSHER, one who strewed the floor with rushes.

RUSSET, homespun cloth of neutral or reddish-brown colour.

SACK, loose, flowing gown.

SADLY, seriously, with gravity.

SAD(NESS), sober, serious(ness).

SAFFI, bailiffs.

ST. THOMAS A WATERINGS, place in Surrey where criminals were executed.

SAKER, small piece of ordnance.

SALT, leap.

SALT, lascivious.

SAMPSUCHINE, sweet marjoram.

SARABAND, a slow dance.

SATURNALS, began December 17.

SAUCINESS, presumption, insolence.

SAUCY, bold, impudent, wanton.

SAUNA (Lat.), a gesture of contempt.

SAVOUR, perceive; gratify, please; to partake of the nature.

SAY, sample.

SAY, assay, try.

SCALD, word of contempt, implying dirt and disease.

SCALLION, shalot, small onion.

SCANDERBAG, "name which the Turks (in allusion to Alexander the Great) gave to the brave Castriot, chief of Albania, with whom they had continual wars. His romantic life had just been translated" (Gifford).

SCAPE, escape.

SCARAB, beetle.

SCARTOCCIO, fold of paper, cover, cartouch, cartridge.

SCONCE, head.

SCOPE, aim.

SCOT AND LOT, tax, contribution (formerly a parish assessment).

SCOTOMY, dizziness in the head.

SCOUR, purge.

SCOURSE, deal, swap.

SCRATCHES, disease of horses.

SCROYLE, mean, rascally fellow.

SCRUPLE, doubt.

SEAL, put hand to the giving up of property or rights.

SEALED, stamped as genuine.

SEAM-RENT, ragged.

SEAMING LACES, insertion or edging.

SEAR UP, close by searing, burning.

SEARCED, sifted.

SECRETARY, able to keep a secret.

SECULAR, worldly, ordinary, commonplace.

SECURE, confident.

SEELIE, happy, blest.

SEISIN, legal term: possession.

SELLARY, lewd person.

SEMBLABLY, similarly.

SEMINARY, a Romish priest educated in a foreign seminary.

SENSELESS, insensible, without sense or feeling.

SENSIBLY, perceptibly.

SENSIVE, sensitive.

SENSUAL, pertaining to the physical or material.

SERENE, harmful dew of evening.

SERICON, red tincture.

SERVANT, lover.

SERVICES, doughty deeds of arms.

SESTERCE, Roman copper coin.

SET, stake, wager.

SET UP, drill.

SETS, deep plaits of the ruff.

SEWER, officer who served up the feast, and brought water for the hands of the guests.

SHAPE, a suit by way of disguise.

SHIFT, fraud, dodge.

SHIFTER, cheat.

SHITTLE, shuttle; "shittle-cock," shuttlecock.

SHOT, tavern reckoning.

SHOT-CLOG, one only tolerated because he paid the shot (reckoning) for the rest.

SHOT-FREE, scot-free, not having to pay.

SHOVE-GROAT, low kind of gambling amusement, perhaps somewhat of the nature of pitch and toss.

SHOT-SHARKS, drawers.

SHREWD, mischievous, malicious, curst.

SHREWDLY, keenly, in a high degree.

SHRIVE, sheriff; posts were set up before his door for proclamations, or to indicate his residence.

SHROVING, Shrovetide, season of merriment.

SIGILLA, seal, mark.

SILENCED BRETHERN, MINISTERS, those of the Church or Nonconformists who had been silenced, deprived, etc.

SILLY, simple, harmless.

SIMPLE, silly, witless; plain, true.

SIMPLES, herbs.

SINGLE, term of chase, signifying when the hunted stag is separated from the herd, or forced to break covert.

SINGLE, weak, silly.

SINGLE-MONEY, small change.

SINGULAR, unique, supreme.

SI-QUIS, bill, advertisement.

SKELDRING, getting money under false pretences; swindling.

SKILL, "it--s not," matters not.

SKINK(ER), pour, draw(er), tapster.

SKIRT, tail.

SLEEK, smooth.

SLICE, fire shovel or pan (dial.).

SLICK, sleek, smooth.

'SLID, 'SLIGHT, 'SPRECIOUS, irreverent oaths.

SLIGHT, sleight, cunning, cleverness; trick.

SLIP, counterfeit coin, bastard.

SLIPPERY, polished and shining.

SLOPS, large loose breeches.

SLOT, print of a stag's foot.

SLUR, put a slur on; cheat (by sliding a die in some way).

SMELT, gull, simpleton.

SNORLE, "perhaps snarl, as Puppy is addressed" (Cunningham).

SNOTTERIE, filth.

SNUFF, anger, resentment; "take in--," take offence at.

SNUFFERS, small open silver dishes for holding snuff, or receptacle for placing snuffers in (Halliwell).

SOCK, shoe worn by comic actors.

SOD, seethe.

SOGGY, soaked, sodden.

SOIL, "take--," said of a hunted stag when he takes to the water for safety.

SOL, sou.

SOLDADOES, soldiers.

SOLICIT, rouse, excite to action.

SOOTH, flattery, cajolery.

SOOTHE, flatter, humour.

SOPHISTICATE, adulterate.

SORT, company, party; rank, degree.

SORT, suit, fit; select.

SOUSE, ear.

SOUSED ("Devil is an Ass"), fol. read "sou't," which Dyce interprets as "a variety of the spelling of "shu'd": to "shu" is to scare a bird away." (See his "Webster," page 350).

SOWTER, cobbler.

SPAGYRICA, chemistry according to the teachings of Paracelsus.

SPAR, bar.

SPEAK, make known, proclaim.

SPECULATION, power of sight.

SPED, to have fared well, prospered.

SPEECE, species.

SPIGHT, anger, rancour.

SPINNER, spider.

SPINSTRY, lewd person.

SPITTLE, hospital, lazar-house.

SPLEEN, considered the seat of the emotions.

SPLEEN, caprice, humour, mood.

SPRUNT, spruce.

SPURGE, foam.

SPUR-RYAL, gold coin worth 15s.

SQUIRE, square, measure; "by the--," exactly.

STAGGERING, wavering, hesitating.

STAIN, disparagement, disgrace.

STALE, decoy, or cover, stalking-horse.

STALE, make cheap, common.

STALK, approach stealthily or under cover.

STALL, forestall.

STANDARD, suit.

STAPLE, market, emporium.

STARK, downright.

STARTING-HOLES, loopholes of escape.

STATE, dignity; canopied chair of state; estate.

STATUMINATE, support vines by poles or stakes; used by Pliny (Gifford).

STAY, gag.

STAY, await; detain.

STICKLER, second or umpire.

STIGMATISE, mark, brand.

STILL, continual(ly), constant(ly).

STINKARD, stinking fellow.

STINT, stop.

STIPTIC, astringent.

STOCCATA, thrust in fencing.

STOCK-FISH, salted and dried fish.

STOMACH, pride, valour.

STOMACH, resent.

STOOP, swoop down as a hawk.

STOP, fill, stuff.

STOPPLE, stopper.

STOTE, stoat, weasel.

STOUP, stoop, swoop=bow.

STRAIGHT, straightway.

STRAMAZOUN (Ital. stramazzone), a down blow, as opposed to the thrust.

STRANGE, like a stranger, unfamiliar.

STRANGENESS, distance of behaviour.

STREIGHTS, OR BERMUDAS, labyrinth of alleys and courts in the Strand.

STRIGONIUM, Grau in Hungary, taken from the Turks in 1597.

STRIKE, balance (accounts).

STRINGHALT, disease of horses.

STROKER, smoother, flatterer.

STROOK, p.p. of "strike."

STRUMMEL-PATCHED, strummel is glossed in dialect dicts. as "a long, loose and dishevelled head of hair."

STUDIES, studious efforts.

STYLE, title; pointed instrument used for writing on wax tablets.

SUBTLE, fine, delicate, thin; smooth, soft.

SUBTLETY (SUBTILITY), subtle device.

SUBURB, connected with loose living.

SUCCUBAE, demons in form of women.

SUCK, extract money from.

SUFFERANCE, suffering.

SUMMED, term of falconry: with full-grown plumage.

SUPER-NEGULUM, topers turned the cup bottom up when it was empty.

SUPERSTITIOUS, over-scrupulous.

SUPPLE, to make pliant.

SURBATE, make sore with walking.

SURCEASE, cease.

SUR-REVERENCE, save your reverence.

SURVISE, peruse.

SUSCITABILITY, excitability.

SUSPECT, suspicion.

SUSPEND, suspect.

SUSPENDED, held over for the present.

SUTLER, victualler.

SWAD, clown, boor.

SWATH BANDS, swaddling clothes.

SWINGE, beat.

TABERD, emblazoned mantle or tunic worn by knights and heralds.

TABLE(S), "pair of--," tablets, note-book.

TABOR, small drum.

TABRET, tabor.

TAFFETA, silk; "tuft-taffeta," a more costly silken fabric.

TAINT, "--a staff," break a lance at tilting in an unscientific or dishonourable manner.

TAKE IN, capture, subdue.

TAKE ME WITH YOU, let me understand you.

TAKE UP, obtain on credit, borrow.

TALENT, sum or weight of Greek currency.

TALL, stout, brave.

TANKARD-BEARERS, men employed to fetch water from the conduits.

TARLETON, celebrated comedian and jester.

TARTAROUS, like a Tartar.

TAVERN-TOKEN, "to swallow a--," get drunk.

TELL, count.

TELL-TROTH, truth-teller.

TEMPER, modify, soften.

TENDER, show regard, care for, cherish; manifest.

TENT, "take--," take heed.

TERSE, swept and polished.

TERTIA, "that portion of an army levied out of one particular district or division of a country" (Gifford).

TESTON, tester, coin worth 6d.

THIRDBOROUGH, constable.

THREAD, quality.

THREAVES, droves.

THREE-FARTHINGS, piece of silver current under Elizabeth.

THREE-PILED, of finest quality, exaggerated.

THRIFTILY, carefully.

THRUMS, ends of the weaver's warp; coarse yarn made from.

THUMB-RING, familiar spirits were supposed capable of being carried about in various ornaments or parts of dress.

TIBICINE, player on the tibia, or pipe.

TICK-TACK, game similar to backgammon.

TIGHTLY, promptly.

TIM, (?) expressive of a climax of nonentity.

TIMELESS, untimely, unseasonable.

TINCTURE, an essential or spiritual principle supposed by alchemists to be transfusible into material things; an imparted characteristic or tendency.

TINK, tinkle.

TIPPET, "turn--," change behaviour or way of life.

TIPSTAFF, staff tipped with metal.

TIRE, head-dress.

TIRE, feed ravenously, like a bird of prey.

TITILLATION, that which tickles the senses, as a perfume.

TOD, fox.

TOILED, worn out, harassed.

TOKEN, piece of base metal used in place of very small coin, when this was scarce.

TONNELS, nostrils.

TOP, "parish--," large top kept in villages for amusement and exercise in frosty weather when people were out of work.

TOTER, tooter, player on a wind instrument.

TOUSE, pull, rend.

TOWARD, docile, apt; on the way to; as regards; present, at hand.

TOY, whim; trick; term of contempt.

TRACT, attraction.

TRAIN, allure, entice.

TRANSITORY, transmittable.

TRANSLATE, transform.

TRAY-TRIP, game at dice (success depended on throwing a three) (Nares).

TREACHOUR (TRECHER), traitor.

TREEN, wooden.

TRENCHER, serving-man who carved or served food.

TRENDLE-TAIL, trundle-tail, curly-tailed.

TRICK (TRICKING), term of heraldry: to draw outline of coat of arms, etc., without blazoning.

TRIG, a spruce, dandified man.

TRILL, trickle.

TRILLIBUB, tripe, any worthless, trifling thing.

TRIPOLY, "come from--," able to perform feats of agility, a "jest nominal," depending on the first part of the word (Gifford).

TRITE, worn, shabby.

TRIVIA, three-faced goddess (Hecate).

TROJAN, familiar term for an equal or inferior; thief.

TROLL, sing loudly.

TROMP, trump, deceive.

TROPE, figure of speech.

TROW, think, believe, wonder.

TROWLE, troll.

TROWSES, breeches, drawers.

TRUCHMAN, interpreter.

TRUNDLE, JOHN, well-known printer.

TRUNDLE, roll, go rolling along.

TRUNDLING CHEATS, term among gipsies and beggars for carts or coaches (Gifford).

TRUNK, speaking-tube.

TRUSS, tie the tagged laces that fastened the breeches to the doublet.

TUBICINE, trumpeter.

TUCKET (Ital. toccato), introductory flourish on the trumpet.

TUITION, guardianship.

TUMBLER, a particular kind of dog so called from the mode of his hunting.

TUMBREL-SLOP, loose, baggy breeches.

TURD, excrement.

TUSK, gnash the teeth (Century Dict.).

TWIRE, peep, twinkle.

TWOPENNY ROOM, gallery.

TYRING-HOUSE, attiring-room.

ULENSPIEGEL. See Howleglass.

UMBRATILE, like or pertaining to a shadow.

UMBRE, brown dye.

UNBATED, unabated.

UNBORED, (?) excessively bored.

UNCARNATE, not fleshly, or of flesh.

UNCOUTH, strange, unusual.

UNDERTAKER, "one who undertook by his influence in the House of Commons to carry things agreeably to his Majesty's wishes" (Whalley); one who becomes surety for.

UNEQUAL, unjust.

UNEXCEPTED, no objection taken at.

UNFEARED, unaffrighted.

UNHAPPILY, unfortunately.

UNICORN'S HORN, supposed antidote to poison.

UNKIND(LY), unnatural(ly).

UNMANNED, untamed (term in falconry).

UNQUIT, undischarged.

UNREADY, undressed.

UNRUDE, rude to an extreme.

UNSEASONED, unseasonable, unripe.

UNSEELED, a hawk's eyes were "seeled" by sewing the eyelids together with fine thread.

UNTIMELY, unseasonably.

UNVALUABLE, invaluable.

UPBRAID, make a matter of reproach.

UPSEE, heavy kind of Dutch beer (Halliwell); "--Dutch," in the Dutch fashion.

UPTAILS ALL, refrain of a popular song.

URGE, allege as accomplice, instigator.

URSHIN, URCHIN, hedgehog.

USE, interest on money; part of sermon dealing with the practical application of doctrine.

USE, be in the habit of, accustomed to; put out to interest.

USQUEBAUGH, whisky.

USURE, usury.

UTTER, put in circulation, make to pass current; put forth for sale.

VAIL, bow, do homage.

VAILS, tips, gratuities.

VALL. See Vail.

VALLIES (Fr. valise), portmanteau, bag.

VAPOUR(S) (n. and v.), used affectedly, like "humour," in many senses, often very vaguely and freely ridiculed by Jonson; humour, disposition, whims, brag(ging), hector(ing), etc.

VARLET, bailiff, or serjeant-at-mace.

VAUT, vault.

VEER (naut.), pay out.

VEGETAL, vegetable; person full of life and vigour.

VELLUTE, velvet.

VELVET CUSTARD. Cf. "Taming of the Shrew," iv. 3, 82, "custard coffin," coffin being the raised crust over a pie.

VENT, vend, sell; give outlet to; scent, snuff up.

VENUE, bout (fencing term).

VERDUGO (Span.), hangman, executioner.

VERGE, "in the--," within a certain distance of the court.

VEX, agitate, torment.

VICE, the buffoon of old moralities; some kind of machinery for moving a puppet (Gifford).

VIE AND REVIE, to hazard a certain sum, and to cover it with a larger one.

VINCENT AGAINST YORK, two heralds-at-arms.

VINDICATE, avenge.

VIRGE, wand, rod.

VIRGINAL, old form of piano.

VIRTUE, valour.

VIVELY, in lifelike manner, livelily.

VIZARD, mask.

VOGUE, rumour, gossip.

VOICE, vote.

VOID, leave, quit.

VOLARY, cage, aviary.

VOLLEY, "at--," "o' the volee," at random (from a term of tennis).

VORLOFFE, furlough.

WADLOE, keeper of the Devil Tavern, where Jonson and his friends met in the 'Apollo' room (Whalley).

WAIGHTS, waits, night musicians, "band of musical watchmen" (Webster), or old form of "hautboys."

WANNION, "vengeance," "plague" (Nares).

WARD, a famous pirate.

WARD, guard in fencing.

WATCHET, pale, sky blue.

WEAL, welfare.

WEED, garment.

WEFT, waif.

WEIGHTS, "to the gold--," to every minute particular.

WELKIN, sky.

WELL-SPOKEN, of fair speech.

WELL-TORNED, turned and polished, as on a wheel.

WELT, hem, border of fur.

WHER, whether.

WHETSTONE, GEORGE, an author who lived 1544(?) to 1587(?).

WHIFF, a smoke, or drink; "taking the--," inhaling the tobacco smoke or some such accomplishment.

WHIGH-HIES, neighings, whinnyings.

WHIMSY, whim, "humour."

WHINILING, (?) whining, weakly.

WHIT, (?) a mere jot.

WHITEMEAT, food made of milk or eggs.

WICKED, bad, clumsy.

WICKER, pliant, agile.

WILDING, esp. fruit of wild apple or crab tree (Webster).

WINE, "I have the--for you," Prov.: I have the perquisites (of the office) which you are to share (Cunningham).

WINNY, "same as old word "wonne," to stay, etc." (Whalley).

WISE-WOMAN, fortune-teller.

WISH, recommend.

WISS (WUSSE), "I--," certainly, of a truth.

WITHOUT, beyond.

WITTY, cunning, ingenious, clever.

WOOD, collection, lot.

WOODCOCK, term of contempt.

WOOLSACK ("--pies"), name of tavern.

WORT, unfermented beer.

WOUNDY, great, extreme.

WREAK, revenge.

WROUGHT, wrought upon.

WUSSE, interjection. (See Wiss).

YEANLING, lamb, kid.

ZANY, an inferior clown, who attended upon the chief fool and mimicked his tricks.

www.bookjungle.com *email: sales@bookjungle.com fax: 630-214-0564 mail: Book Jungle PO Box 2226 Champaign, IL 61825*

The Codes Of Hammurabi And Moses
W. W. Davies

QTY

The discovery of the Hammurabi Code is one of the greatest achievements of archaeology, and is of paramount interest, not only to the student of the Bible, but also to all those interested in ancient history...

Religion   **ISBN:** *1-59462-338-4*   **Pages:** 132
MSRP $12.95

The Theory of Moral Sentiments
Adam Smith

QTY

This work from 1749. contains original theories of conscience amd moral judgment and it is the foundation for systemof morals.

Philosophy   **ISBN:** *1-59462-777-0*   **Pages:** 536
MSRP $19.95

Jessica's First Prayer
Hesba Stretton

QTY

In a screened and secluded corner of one of the many railway-bridges which span the streets of London there could be seen a few years ago, from five o'clock every morning until half past eight, a tidily set-out coffee-stall, consisting of a trestle and board, upon which stood two large tin cans, with a small fire of charcoal burning under each so as to keep the coffee boiling during the early hours of the morning when the work-people were thronging into the city on their way to their daily toil...

Pages: 84

Childrens   **ISBN:** *1-59462-373-2*   *MSRP $9.95*

My Life and Work
Henry Ford

QTY

Henry Ford revolutionized the world with his implementation of mass production for the Model T automobile. Gain valuable business insight into his life and work with his own auto-biography... "We have only started on our development of our country we have not as yet, with all our talk of wonderful progress, done more than scratch the surface. The progress has been wonderful enough but..."

Pages: 300

Biographies/   **ISBN:** *1-59462-198-5*   *MSRP $21.95*

www.bookjungle.com *email: sales@bookjungle.com fax: 630-214-0564 mail: Book Jungle PO Box 2226 Champaign, IL 61825*

The Art of Cross-Examination
Francis Wellman

QTY

I presume it is the experience of every author, after his first book is published upon an important subject, to be almost overwhelmed with a wealth of ideas and illustrations which could readily have been included in his book, and which to his own mind, at least, seem to make a second edition inevitable. Such certainly was the case with me; and when the first edition had reached its sixth impression in five months, I rejoiced to learn that it seemed to my publishers that the book had met with a sufficiently favorable reception to justify a second and considerably enlarged edition. ..

Reference   ISBN: *1-59462-647-2*   Pages:412   MSRP *$19.95*

On the Duty of Civil Disobedience
Henry David Thoreau

QTY

Thoreau wrote his famous essay, On the Duty of Civil Disobedience, as a protest against an unjust but popular war and the immoral but popular institution of slave-owning. He did more than write he declined to pay his taxes, and was hauled off to gaol in consequence. Who can say how much this refusal of his hastened the end of the war and of slavery ?

Law   ISBN: *1-59462-747-9*   Pages:48   MSRP *$7.45*

Dream Psychology Psychoanalysis for Beginners
Sigmund Freud

QTY

Sigmund Freud, born Sigismund Schlomo Freud (May 6, 1856 - September 23, 1939), was a Jewish-Austrian neurologist and psychiatrist who co-founded the psychoanalytic school of psychology. Freud is best known for his theories of the unconscious mind, especially involving the mechanism of repression; his redefinition of sexual desire as mobile and directed towards a wide variety of objects; and his therapeutic techniques, especially his understanding of transference in the therapeutic relationship and the presumed value of dreams as sources of insight into unconscious desires.

Psychology   ISBN: *1-59462-905-6*   Pages:196   MSRP *$15.45*

The Miracle of Right Thought
Orison Swett Marden

QTY

Believe with all of your heart that you will do what you were made to do. When the mind has once formed the habit of holding cheerful, happy, prosperous pictures, it will not be easy to form the opposite habit. It does not matter how improbable or how far away this realization may see, or how dark the prospects may be, if we visualize them as best we can, as vividly as possible, hold tenaciously to them and vigorously struggle to attain them, they will gradually become actualized, realized in the life. But a desire, a longing without endeavor, a yearning abandoned or held indifferently will vanish without realization.

Self Help   ISBN: *1-59462-644-8*   Pages:360   MSRP *$25.45*

www.bookjungle.com *email: sales@bookjungle.com fax: 630-214-0564 mail: Book Jungle PO Box 2226 Champaign, IL 61825*

QTY

☐ **The Rosicrucian Cosmo-Conception Mystic Christianity** *by* **Max Heindel**   ISBN: *1-59462-188-8*   **$38.95**
The Rosicrucian Cosmo-conception is not dogmatic, neither does it appeal to any other authority than the reason of the student. It is: not controversial, but is: sent forth in the, hope that it may help to clear...
New Age/Religion Pages 646

☐ **Abandonment To Divine Providence** *by* **Jean-Pierre de Caussade**   ISBN: *1-59462-228-0*   **$25.95**
"The Rev. Jean Pierre de Caussade was one of the most remarkable spiritual writers of the Society of Jesus in France in the 18th Century. His death took place at Toulouse in 1751. His works have gone through many editions and have been republished...
Inspirational/Religion Pages 400

☐ **Mental Chemistry** *by* **Charles Haanel**   ISBN: *1-59462-192-6*   **$23.95**
Mental Chemistry allows the change of material conditions by combining and appropriately utilizing the power of the mind. Much like applied chemistry creates something new and unique out of careful combinations of chemicals the mastery of mental chemistry...
New Age Pages 354

☐ **The Letters of Robert Browning and Elizabeth Barret Barrett 1845-1846 vol II**   ISBN: *1-59462-193-4*   **$35.95**
by **Robert Browning** *and* **Elizabeth Barrett**
Biographies Pages 596

☐ **Gleanings In Genesis (volume I)** *by* **Arthur W. Pink**   ISBN: *1-59462-130-6*   **$27.45**
Appropriately has Genesis been termed "the seed plot of the Bible" for in it we have, in germ form, almost all of the great doctrines which are afterwards fully developed in the books of Scripture which follow...
Religion/Inspirational Pages 420

☐ **The Master Key** *by* **L. W. de Laurence**   ISBN: *1-59462-001-6*   **$30.95**
In no branch of human knowledge has there been a more lively increase of the spirit of research during the past few years than in the study of Psychology, Concentration and Mental Discipline. The requests for authentic lessons in Thought Control, Mental Discipline and...
New Age/Business Pages 422

☐ **The Lesser Key Of Solomon Goetia** *by* **L. W. de Laurence**   ISBN: *1-59462-092-X*   **$9.95**
This translation of the first book of the "Lernegton" which is now for the first time made accessible to students of Talismanic Magic was done, after careful collation and edition, from numerous Ancient Manuscripts in Hebrew, Latin, and French...
New Age/Occult Pages 92

☐ **Rubaiyat Of Omar Khayyam** *by* **Edward Fitzgerald**   ISBN: *1-59462-332-5*   **$13.95**
Edward Fitzgerald, whom the world has already learned, in spite of his own efforts to remain within the shadow of anonymity, to look upon as one of the rarest poets of the century, was born at Bredfield, in Suffolk, on the 31st of March, 1809. He was the third son of John Purcell...
Music Pages 172

☐ **Ancient Law** *by* **Henry Maine**   ISBN: *1-59462-128-4*   **$29.95**
The chief object of the following pages is to indicate some of the earliest ideas of mankind, as they are reflected in Ancient Law, and to point out the relation of those ideas to modern thought.
Religion/History Pages 452

☐ **Far-Away Stories** *by* **William J. Locke**   ISBN: *1-59462-129-2*   **$19.45**
"Good wine needs no bush, but a collection of mixed vintages does. And this book is just such a collection. Some of the stories I do not want to remain buried for ever in the museum files of dead magazine-numbers an author's not unpardonable vanity..."
Fiction Pages 272

☐ **Life of David Crockett** *by* **David Crockett**   ISBN: *1-59462-250-7*   **$27.45**
"Colonel David Crockett was one of the most remarkable men of the times in which he lived. Born in humble life, but gifted with a strong will, an indomitable courage, and unremitting perseverance...
Biographies/New Age Pages 424

☐ **Lip-Reading** *by* **Edward Nitchie**   ISBN: *1-59462-206-X*   **$25.95**
Edward B. Nitchie, founder of the New York School for the Hard of Hearing, now the Nitchie School of Lip-Reading, Inc, wrote "LIP-READING Principles and Practice". The development and perfecting of this meritorious work on lip-reading was an undertaking...
How-to Pages 400

☐ **A Handbook of Suggestive Therapeutics, Applied Hypnotism, Psychic Science**   ISBN: *1-59462-214-0*   **$24.95**
by **Henry Munro**
Health/New Age/Health/Self-help Pages 376

☐ **A Doll's House: and Two Other Plays** *by* **Henrik Ibsen**   ISBN: *1-59462-112-8*   **$19.95**
Henrik Ibsen created this classic when in revolutionary 1848 Rome. Introducing some striking concepts in playwriting for the realist genre, this play has been studied the world over.
Fiction/Classics/Plays 308

☐ **The Light of Asia** *by* **sir Edwin Arnold**   ISBN: *1-59462-204-3*   **$13.95**
In this poetic masterpiece, Edwin Arnold describes the life and teachings of Buddha. The man who was to become known as Buddha to the world was born as Prince Gautama of India but he rejected the worldly riches and abandoned the reigns of power when...
Religion/History/Biographies Pages 170

☐ **The Complete Works of Guy de Maupassant** *by* **Guy de Maupassant**   ISBN: *1-59462-157-8*   **$16.95**
"For days and days, nights and nights, I had dreamed of that first kiss which was to consecrate our engagement, and I knew not on what spot I should put my lips..."
Fiction/Classics Pages 240

☐ **The Art of Cross-Examination** *by* **Francis L. Wellman**   ISBN: *1-59462-309-0*   **$26.95**
Written by a renowned trial lawyer, Wellman imparts his experience and uses case studies to explain how to use psychology to extract desired information through questioning.
How-to/Science/Reference Pages 408

☐ **Answered or Unanswered?** *by* **Louisa Vaughan**   ISBN: *1-59462-248-5*   **$10.95**
Miracles of Faith in China
Religion Pages 112

☐ **The Edinburgh Lectures on Mental Science (1909)** *by* **Thomas**   ISBN: *1-59462-008-3*   **$11.95**
This book contains the substance of a course of lectures recently given by the writer in the Queen Street Hail, Edinburgh. Its purpose is to indicate the Natural Principles governing the relation between Mental Action and Material Conditions...
New Age/Psychology Pages 148

☐ **Ayesha** *by* **H. Rider Haggard**   ISBN: *1-59462-301-5*   **$24.95**
Verily and indeed it is the unexpected that happens! Probably if there was one person upon the earth from whom the Editor of this, and of a certain previous history, did not expect to hear again...
Classics Pages 380

☐ **Ayala's Angel** *by* **Anthony Trollope**   ISBN: *1-59462-352-X*   **$29.95**
The two girls were both pretty, but Lucy who was twenty-one who supposed to be simple and comparatively unattractive, whereas Ayala was credited, as her Bombwhat romantic name might show, with poetic charm and a taste for romance. Ayala when her father died was nineteen...
Fiction Pages 484

☐ **The American Commonwealth** *by* **James Bryce**   ISBN: *1-59462-286-8*   **$34.45**
An interpretation of American democratic political theory. It examines political mechanics and society from the perspective of Scotsman James Bryce
Politics Pages 572

☐ **Stories of the Pilgrims** *by* **Margaret P. Pumphrey**   ISBN: *1-59462-116-0*   **$17.95**
This book explores pilgrims religious oppression in England as well as their escape to Holland and eventual crossing to America on the Mayflower, and their early days in New England...
History Pages 268

www.bookjungle.com email: sales@bookjungle.com fax: 630-214-0564 mail: Book Jungle PO Box 2226 Champaign, IL 61825

			QTY
The Fasting Cure by *Sinclair Upton*	ISBN: *1-59462-222-1*	**$13.95**	☐
In the Cosmopolitan Magazine for May, 1910, and in the Contemporary Review (London) for April, 1910, I published an article dealing with my experiences in fasting. I have written a great many magazine articles, but never one which attracted so much attention...		New Age/Self Help/Health Pages 164	
Hebrew Astrology by *Sepharial*	ISBN: *1-59462-308-2*	**$13.45**	☐
In these days of advanced thinking it is a matter of common observation that we have left many of the old landmarks behind and that we are now pressing forward to greater heights and to a wider horizon than that which represented the mind-content of our progenitors...		Astrology Pages 144	
Thought Vibration or The Law of Attraction in the Thought World	ISBN: *1-59462-127-6*	**$12.95**	☐
by *William Walker Atkinson*		Psychology/Religion Pages 144	
Optimism by *Helen Keller*	ISBN: *1-59462-108-X*	**$15.95**	☐
Helen Keller was blind, deaf, and mute since 19 months old, yet famously learned how to overcome these handicaps, communicate with the world, and spread her lectures promoting optimism. An inspiring read for everyone...		Biographies/Inspirational Pages 84	
Sara Crewe by *Frances Burnett*	ISBN: *1-59462-360-0*	**$9.45**	☐
In the first place, Miss Minchin lived in London. Her home was a large, dull, tall one, in a large, dull square, where all the houses were alike, and all the sparrows were alike, and where all the door-knockers made the same heavy sound...		Childrens/Classic Pages 88	
The Autobiography of Benjamin Franklin by *Benjamin Franklin*	ISBN: *1-59462-135-7*	**$24.95**	☐
The Autobiography of Benjamin Franklin has probably been more extensively read than any other American historical work, and no other book of its kind has had such ups and downs of fortune. Franklin lived for many years in England, where he was agent...		Biographies/History Pages 332	

Name	
Email	
Telephone	
Address	
City, State ZIP	

☐ Credit Card   ☐ Check / Money Order

Credit Card Number	
Expiration Date	
Signature	

Please Mail to: Book Jungle
                    PO Box 2226
                    Champaign, IL 61825
or Fax to: 630-214-0564

ORDERING INFORMATION
web: www.bookjungle.com
email: sales@bookjungle.com
fax: 630-214-0564
mail: Book Jungle PO Box 2226 Champaign, IL 61825
or PayPal to sales@bookjungle.com

Please contact us for bulk discounts

DIRECT-ORDER TERMS

20% Discount if You Order Two or More Books
Free Domestic Shipping!
Accepted: Master Card, Visa, Discover, American Express

www.ingramcontent.com/pod-product-compliance
Lightning Source LLC
Chambersburg PA
CBHW080532170426
43195CB00016B/2539